WHEN INDIA VOTES

Professor Jaishri Jethwaney, with a Ph.D. in Media and Elections from the School of International Studies, Jawaharlal Nehru University, worked at the premier Indian Institute of Mass Communication (IIMC) as professor and programme director (Advertising and Public Relations) for more than a quarter of a century. She has authored a number of textbooks, including those on corporate communication and social sector communication, and co-authored those on advertising management, among many others.

Dr Jethwaney is part of the Institute for Studies in Industrial Development (ISID), a policy research institute under Indian Council of Social Science Research (ICSSR), as a visiting professor since January 2017. She is currently Project Director for a seminal policy research on advertising. She is also on the boards of studies and academic councils of various universities and institutes of higher learning.

Dr Jethwaney is a well-known corporate trainer in various areas of management, including corporate communication, media, disaster management and crisis communication.

Dr Samir Kapur, an engineer, MBA and Ph.D., is a versatile professional with over twenty years of experience. He is currently working as part of the senior management team at Adfactors PR, India's largest public relations agency. He has strategized and executed multiple public relations, international relations, advocacy and marketing campaigns for various political parties and prominent development sectors, leading Indian conglomerates and multinational companies. He is a visiting faculty and in the academic councils of various management colleges. Dr Kapur has coached numerous senior executives and politicians on media interactions and message delivery.

WHEN INDIA VOTES

THE DYNAMICS OF SUCCESSFUL ELECTION CAMPAIGNING

Jaishri Jethwaney & Samir Kapur

RUPA

Published by
Rupa Publications India Pvt. Ltd 2019
7/16, Ansari Road, Daryaganj
New Delhi 110002

Sales Centres:
Allahabad Bengaluru Chennai
Hyderabad Jaipur Kathmandu
Kolkata Mumbai

Copyright © Jaishri Jethwaney and Samir Kapur 2019

The views and opinions expressed in this book are the author's own and the facts are as reported by him which have been verified to the extent possible, and the publishers are not in any way liable for the same. Names of some people have been changed to protect their privacy.

All rights reserved.
No part of this publication may be reproduced, transmitted, or stored in a retrieval system, in any form or by any means, electronic, mechanical, photocopying, recording or otherwise, without the prior permission of the publisher.

ISBN: 978-93-5333-380-5

First impression 2019

10 9 8 7 6 5 4 3 2 1

The moral right of the author has been asserted.

Printed by Nutech Print Services, Faridabad

This book is sold subject to the condition that it shall not, by way of trade or otherwise, be lent, resold, hired out, or otherwise circulated, without the publisher's prior consent, in any form of binding or cover other than that in which it is published.

To the astute Indian electorate and political parties that have contributed to making India one of the most-talked-about liberal democracies.

CONTENTS

1. Mass Media, Public Opinion and Democracy — 1
2. Media in India: Imperatives for Election Campaigning — 20
3. Media Objectivity: Reality or Myth? — 49
4. The Incongruent Millions as Voters and Media Audiences: Impact on Elections — 72
5. Ideas, Ideologies and Campaign Planks: Deconstructing Election Campaigns 1984–2014 — 105
6. The Sixteenth Parliamentary Elections: The Mother of All Elections; the Emergence of Modi the Campaigner — 141
7. Discussion: Mapping the Changes on India's Political Landscape — 180

Acknowledgments — 199
Index — 201

1

MASS MEDIA, PUBLIC OPINION AND DEMOCRACY

> 'I understand democracy as something that gives the weak the same chance as the strong.'
>
> —MAHATMA GANDHI

'*Vox populi vox dei*,' an oft-quoted axiom in democracies, was coined by the Greeks and conveyed that the voice of the people was indeed the voice of God. Democracy is the manifestation of people's will to be governed by those they elect. It is a different matter that the very same people as voters may not necessarily be happy with the elected representatives they choose to govern them. Democracy, also, is not necessarily the voice of the majority. Many people do not vote, and those who do may not see their candidates win.

Society has a history spanning millions of years, and the media, especially the mass media, is a little over a century old. Yet it is ironical that the media, over the years, has accumulated immense power to influence society in more ways than one. The media's power comes from its capacity to influence public opinion. Media critics believe that it is not a knowledge-based profession, but depends on events and happenings interpreted from both the supply side of information—through press releases, backgrounders, press conferences, events, etc.—and the demand side of information, from the perspective of reporters who interpret events and information according to their understanding and mental capability. The media, therefore, can be seen as a social institution, which is not and cannot be very different from the nature of the society it exists in.

The relationship between the media and society is symbiotic. In fact, any debate on the mass media and society oscillates between two extremes, depending on who is saying it. Some swear by the media's unbridled power, while others feel that the media does not affect lives at all. Whatever may be the cliché in these views, there is no gainsaying the fact that the media has become part of the everyday life of an average person, who makes sense of the world around him/her through media stimuli.

In this chapter, an effort has been made to provide a theoretical construct to the interrelation of democracy, the media and its impact on elections. The last century or so has seen the development of many theories and models around the subject, which have also been tested in many elections in the West, especially in the United States (US). Over the years, elections in other democracies, especially in the developing world, have copied campaign styles and media usage from their Western counterparts, again the US in particular. Critics have often called this the 'Americanization' of elections. There may not have been many scholarly research studies on the Indian elections with a theoretical construct in the past, but the current crop of scholars—from not only India but also the West—has evinced great interest in the Indian elections, and one does find references in contemporary literature on the subject. The later chapters have cited a number of such studies.

British communication theorist Denis McQuail ascribes four important attributes to the mass media that lend it significance.[1]

- **A power source:** The media is the primary means of transmission and source of information in society.
- **The media is in the area of public affairs:** Government organizations and the corporate sector, because of various regulations, are often in the media glare.
- **A definition of social reality:** The media is a forum where the changing culture and values of society and groups are 'constructed, stored and visibly expressed'.
- **A primary key to fame and celebrity status:** First, it was people from the entertainment industry, then sportspersons, and now even corporate honchos, who have acquired celebrity status in the media.

The power of the media, however, is not intrinsic but acquired. This power comes from the people, as consumers and audiences of news and various other programmes. The political institutions that are accountable to the people in a democracy through periodic elections obviously face the worst of a vocal and negative media, and that is what lends power to the media.

Harwood L. Childs, author of *An Introduction to Public Opinion*, in his thesis on the subject, strongly advocates the preserving of public opinion, because many forces in his view seem to be at work, curtailing and undermining its role. These, according to Childs, include the tremendous growth in executive power, the growing complexity and speed of social change, the emergence of pressure groups and higher stakes among political parties, the mass media and other channels.[2]

Representative bodies are becoming less representative, and elections, though they indicate the preferred candidates, often give only a slight indication of public attitude. A section of analysts feels that the decision of the voters is more often shaped by the mass media stimuli around election time. Excessive visibility of certain candidates in comparison to others, cunning campaigns by parties and the 'public face' as presented have the capability to swing public opinion in favour of or against a candidate, which may have nothing to do with the 'real' choice of the electorate, as it should have been. To what extent an average person depends on media messages or to what extent the media shapes our minds, attitudes and opinions is, however, a moot point.

Media and politics

There have been numerous debates leading to concern and anxiety about the increasing role and influence of the media, which, it is alleged, has changed the very fabric of politics. A fascinating, and at times intriguing, interplay of the mass media and politics has been the subject matter of much empirical research.

Politics as an institution has a long history. Many things have influenced politics over the years. Similarly, the media has undergone changes and entered various phases. Political institutions have taken centuries to be what they are today. The media as an institution has progressed in a much shorter period, as said earlier. Thanks to the ingenuity of the human mind, coupled with science and technology, the media has acquired such a formidable position and influence from being a watchdog that it questions institutions and practices that are as old as the human civilization itself. While the news media has historically been viewed as aggressive and overenthusiastic for the latest and hottest information, its watchdog function in a democratic society posits that people know what their governments and public-funded institutions are doing. The media has the power to hold the government and public-funded institutions accountable, forcing them to explain actions and decisions, all of which affect the people they represent. The assumption is that the press speaks for the people, thus the freedom of speech and freedom of the press Acts are widely prevalent in some democracies. The need for freedom of the media is to ensure that it articulates the voice of the people and their concerns by bringing them in the public domain. The argument supports that the news media must question the government, thereby contributing in making democracy function. Therefore, it is important to understand that the freedom of speech and expression is in the interest of the public, and such legislation does not only protect the functions of the press, but also lets it function without fear or favour. Today, in the era of globalization, this role has undergone a sea change. It is often alleged that the media today has become a commodity. There is also growing criticism against the media for projecting unabashed violence. According to Leftist thinking, the media works as a tool to serve the specific socioeconomic and political interests of the dominant classes. The media, the thinking posits, is essentially an instrument for maintaining the hegemony of the dominant classes.

Walter Lippmann, a renowned American journalist and political analyst in the early twentieth century, questioned the purity and adequacy of the mass media as a source of information. He argued that journalists pointed just a 'flashlight' rather than a mirror to the world. Hence, the audience received only selective glimpses and not a complete image of the scene. Lippmann explained why the media could not possibly perform the functions of public enlightenment that the democratic theory required it to. Media persons, he argued, could not tell the truth objectively, because truth was subjective and required more probing investigations and analysis than the busy pace of news production could allow.[3]

Considering news as a puzzle, Harry S. Truman, the late US president, once lamented the role of the media thus, 'I really look with commiseration over the great body of my fellow citizens who, reading newspapers, live and die in the belief that they have known something of what has been passing in the world in their time.'[4]

In the first quarter of the twentieth century, the belief that the media had a powerful impact on the human mind came from the premise that the society was divided between a large populace and a small elite class that was able to manipulate it. This emanated from external events—the impressive rise of the mass press, the radio and moving pictures on the one hand, and the emergence of many political movements on the other. Fascist regimes using the mass media as a tool of propaganda also reinforced this belief.[5]

Media academic Stanley J. Baran, in his book *Introduction to Mass Communication: Media Literacy and Culture*, quoted theorist Marshall McLuhan to explain the importance of the mass media in our lives. McLuhan would often ask, 'Does a fish know it's wet?' The answer, he would say, was an emphatic 'No!'. The existence of the fish is so dominated by water that only when water is absent does it become aware of its condition. So it is with people and the mass media. An average person is so inundated with media messages in his/her everyday life that he/she is often unconscious of the media's presence, not to mention its influence. Various scholars and critics have argued that the media is not only a mirror to society but also an instrument of social change. The media, therefore, must take a close look at society in all its manifestations with a penetrating eye.

Interdependence of democracy, media and public opinion

Democracy, mass media and public opinion are interdependent in the true sense. If we were to look back at history throughout the nineteenth century, when penny press newspapers hit the streets, the potential of the mass media was felt—and dreaded. By seeking the sensational, and concentrating on newsworthy personalities rather than on the news, the press, it was thought, was diverting the attention of the masses, arousing irrational passions and lowering the standards of political debate. However, it was not until the First World War—when the government used the mass media to conduct news management and unleash propaganda—that it was realized that the mass media was indeed an important tool. Hence the interdependence of mass media and propaganda was established.

The success of propaganda led to widespread acceptance by social scientists of the hypodermic needle theory, also known as the magic bullet theory, propounded by American political scientist and communications theorist Harold Dwight Lasswell in 1935. The theory assumed that everyone was exposed to the media message equally. Everyone interpreted the messages in the same general way and the messages affected everyone uniformly. Thus, a cleverly designed message could produce a uniform response from everyone in the population. People were assumed to be 'uniformly controlled by their biologically based "instincts" and, therefore, reacted more or less uniformly to whatever "stimuli" came along'.[6] The hypodermic needle theory was not based on empirical research but reflected the social and psychological theories of the day, which posited that information was transmitted directly from the mass media to the individual, without taking into account the social context within which the message was received. The theory also posited that the individual in modern society, prone to be manipulated, was irrational and governed by unreasonable passion—traits that were a threat to society.[7]

Austrian-American sociologist Paul Felix Lazarsfeld and his colleagues conducted a research study during the election of Franklin D. Roosevelt in 1940 to determine the voting patterns and relationship between the media and political power. The findings revealed that the majority of the public did not seem to be affected by propaganda surrounding Roosevelt's campaign. Instead, the interpersonal route proved more influential than the media. Therefore, it was concluded that the effects of the campaign were not powerful to the point that they completely persuaded the 'helpless audiences', a claim that the hypodermic needle theory and Lasswell asserted. These new findings also suggested that the public was capable of selecting those messages that went with their own beliefs and experiences.[8]

An important observation that emerged from this research was that the respondents, when asked to report on their recent exposure to campaign communication, more often referred to a political discussion rather than to the mass media, such as the print or the radio. This led to the concept of 'opinion leader', and a new hypothesis, the 'two-step flow' of communication, was discovered. The hypothesis posited that opinion leaders, who later transmitted the information to the audience, first absorbed information from the mass media. The opinion leaders were found to be dispersed throughout the social structure and were not necessarily formal leaders. These opinion leaders had more access to mass media campaigns than non-leaders. In fact, the opinion leaders worked as mediators or the intervening variables between the mass media and other people in the group. While the two-step-flow hypothesis received support from sociologists in the 1950s and 1960s[9], psychologists were looking for the effect of the media from the point of view of individual impact.

Joseph Klapper's summary of survey and social psychological research on media effects proposed the reinforcement theory, which added a psychological dimension to the two-step-flow theory. Klapper, known for his influential work in media effects and a career in private broadcasting with CBS, suggested that people avoided access to media messages that were in conflict with their predisposition. From this point of view, psychological mechanisms worked as the intervening variables between the media messages and the audience response. The individual, Klapper felt, was protected in two ways from direct manipulation by the media. On the one hand, the media messages were received indirectly through the opinion leaders and group affiliations, and on the other, psychological predisposition selected only those messages that the receiver found 'congenial' and matching with his/her value system. This played a part in decision-making. In short, what Klapper tried to arrive at was that the mass media functioned among and through multiple and intertwining mediating factors and influences. Most of the time, the media, according to this thesis, reinforced existing conditions, rather than produce new ones. The impact, therefore, was limited.[10]

To illustrate the point further, if a voter was predisposed to vote for a certain candidate or a party, he/she would use the mass media to reinforce his/her political choice. People exercised what the researchers termed 'selective exposure and selective attention'. In other words, when people read newspapers or followed the radio or the television, they paid more attention to information that reinforced their preconceived ideas and dismissed that which contradicted those ideas. But where did the preconceived ideas come from? Political attitudes and voting patterns were heavily determined by community, family and group affiliations, observed the researchers. The transmitted political beliefs of groups held the loyalty of their membership and acted as a buffer against the direct impact of the media. It was called the era of 'minimal effects', meaning that the media in itself was virtually powerless to change minds, that it was rather in the context of family, friends, colleagues and co-workers that it was primarily responsible for people's attitudes and opinions. The hypothesis was formulated during early research into voting behaviour between the 1940s and the 1960s, and this period formed the initial 'minimal effects' era in the US.[11] Later-day scholars, especially in the 1980s, have contested the 'minimal effect' theory and argued that voters did have uncertainties about various candidates' positions and that these uncertainties influence their voting decisions.[12]

The 'agenda-setting' theory tested by Max McCombs and Donald Shaw, journalism professors at the University of North Carolina, spoke of the 'ability (of the news media) to influence the salience of topics on the public agenda'.[13] The agenda-setting theory can also be traced in the works of Lippmann in his 1922 book *Public Opinion*, without using the term. Lippmann argued that the mass media was the major connection between events in the world and the images in the public mind. Following Lippmann, in 1963, Bernard S. Cohen argued that the news media 'may not be successful much of the time in telling people what to think, but it is stunningly successful in telling its readers what to think about. The world will look different to different people.' In the 1960s, Cohen had expressed the idea that later led to the formalization of the agenda-setting theory by McCombs and Shaw.[14]

In the 1968 Chapel Hill study, McCombs and Shaw demonstrated a strong correlation coefficient between what hundred residents of Chapel Hill, North Carolina, thought was the most important election issue and what the news media reported it to be. By comparing the news content with the public's perceptions, McCombs and Shaw were able to discover to what degree the media determined public opinion. Since the study, published in the 1972 edition of the journal *Public Opinion Quarterly*, it is no wonder that hundreds of researches have been published on the agenda-setting function of the mass media, and the theory continues to be regarded as relevant.[15]

Of the various models and theories, Martin Harrop's model has been widely debated and accepted. Harrop identified three models of voter behaviour:[16]

- Party identification model
- Radical model
- Issue model

The party identification model stresses the importance of family socialization as a mechanism linking social cleavages to individual choice. It suggests that party identification is passed from parents to children, along with other loyalties. Partnership strengthens with age, sustained by interactions with people of similar views, as electors come to rely on their allegiance to solve the problem of interpreting complex political information.

The radical model postulates that people vote according to their social interests, though political parties and the mass media both influence the interpretation of these interests.

The issue model treats the voter as an informed citizen, choosing between parties based on which comes closest to or is least distant from his/her own conception of what a government should do. The model looks at voters acting individually and not collectively or expressively. The broad concept of issues can be divided into three parts—the party's ideology, the party's specific policies and the party's competence.

According to Harrop's thesis, the mass media plays a major role in the radical model of voting. Television and the press are believed to define what counts as acceptable political view, to influence citizens into similar modes of thinking to create a stream of messages that can favour one particular party. By contrast, the party identification model views the media as just a reinforcing influence on voting decisions, providing materials that are selectively interpreted by the voters, whose standing commitment to a party insulates them from the effects of the media. In the issue voting model, the media is seen more as a source of information than of value. The reinforcement interpretation of the media is no longer an adequate guide to media effects. Here the party identification model is rather weak. According to his thesis, the media can influence voting behaviour in four situations:

- When party loyalties are weak
- When there are new subjects to cover
- When the coverage is credible
- When people rarely discuss politics

Television, according to Harrop, strengthened the credibility of the media and supplanted conversation as a major channel of political communication. Paid media space through advertising, with its slick messages and imagery, and the news media, with its reportage and editorial comments, have the capability to inform, educate, reinforce and create stereotypes in the minds of the audience. As media messages peak during election time, people as voters are bound to play a part in the generated stimuli.

Since the last quarter of the twentieth century, a large number of political scientists, sociologists and mass communication researchers have believed that the mass media exerts a great power not only in shaping political attitudes and approaches, but also in instructing 'how to think about the world'. The media today, it is generally believed, not only provides information but also the conceptual framework within which information and opinions are ordered. In other words, the receiver gets not just facts but a worldview about the issue. Contemporary media scholars have emphasized the agenda-setting function of the media, an area that for long was in the domain of political parties and governments. As mentioned before, the mass media, analysts believe, may not be as successful in telling people what to think, but it is very successful in telling them what to think about, by laying more stress on certain issues and personalities in prime-time bulletins and providing crucial space in newspapers.

Analysing the evidence of effects, McQuail argues that much of what has been written about the effects or the impact of the media is either based on research on campaigns or involves predictions about hypothetical campaign situations, which include political and election campaign, advertising and public service information, etc. These campaigns may not be popular with the audience, so they invariably have to be 'sold' to them with smart strategies, keeping in view the 'desired response' from the audience.

Gatekeeping function of the mass media

The term 'gatekeeper' was first employed by the German psychologist Kurt Lewin to refer to individuals or a group of persons who govern the flow of information. A gatekeeper can be a film producer who cuts a scene from the original script or a network censor who deletes a scene from a prime-time show because it may be perceived by him/her as provocative, politically incorrect or sexually explicit. A director who determines which segment of film to use in a documentary, a newspaper executive who determines the topic for an editorial or any other individual in charge of the processing or the control of messages disseminated through the mass media can be believed to be exercising the gatekeeping function.

In a nutshell, there are three functions of the gatekeeper:

- To limit the information that the audience/reader receives by editing the information before it is disseminated to them.
- To expand the information the reader/audience receives by giving them additional facts or views.
- To reorganize or reinterpret the information.

The gatekeeping function gives the gatekeeper the choice of sharing or withholding certain information from the audience. This postulates that the mass media is subjective, because it is the gatekeepers who decide what to share, how much to share and what not to share at all. So the claim of the media being objective becomes disputable.

Martin Haselmayer, Markus Wagner and Thomas M. Meyer in their scholarly research paper "Partisan Bias in Message Selection: Media Gatekeeping of Party Press Releases", which first appeared online in August 2017, tested the gatekeeping model with the premise that political parties tried to shape media coverage in ways that were favourable to them, but what determined whether media outlets would pick up and report on party messages was based on not just news factors but also partisan bias. The media was, therefore, more likely to report on messages from parties their readers favoured. Importantly, this effect was greater, rather than weaker, when these messages had high news value.[17] If the newsmaker was powerful and popular, chances were that the news media would likely give more importance to that than the less-popular ones. The researchers worked on three hypotheses that were, in the end, validated. The model was built on two explanatory variables: news value and partisan bias. Thus, journalists were more likely to report on political messages if they had a higher news value (Hypothesis 1). Moreover, journalists were more likely to pay attention to messages from political actors they (and their readership) favoured (Hypothesis 2). Finally, they hypothesized that these two factors interacted in determining media selection of political messages, indicating that the effect of partisan bias on media reporting was conditional on the news value of the political message. Thus, journalists were particularly likely to choose messages of political actors they favoured if those messages also had a high news value (Hypothesis 3). Based on content analyses of 1,496 party press releases and 6,512 media reports from the 2013 Austrian parliamentary election campaign, the researchers demonstrated that media coverage of individual party messages was influenced not just by news factors but also by partisan bias.[18]

Four major theories of the press

In 1956, communication scholars Fred S. Siebert, Theodore Peterson and Wilbur Schramm wrote *Four Theories of the Press*, which went on to become milestones in the study of journalism and communication. A brief analysis of these theories will help one understand more clearly and lucidly the interrelation of the media and society.

The Authoritarian Theory: This assumes that all kinds of communication are under the direct control of the ruling class. It is a necessity to curb the media in order to maintain political hegemony. In addition, the press is an instrument to shape public opinion in favour of the ruling class. The authorities reserve all rights to provide licences to the media and make certain censorships. In case any medium violates the government guidelines, the authority can cancel its licence. The government also has the right to censor any issue from the press to maintain law and order. In short, in an authoritarian dispensation, the media only has as much freedom as the leadership of the ruling class will permit.

The Libertarian Theory: This concept can be traced back to England and the American colonies of the seventeenth century. The basic premise of this theory is the assumption that man is a rational animal with inherent natural rights and, hence, should be given the right to pursue truth. The legacy of this press movement is rich, which includes the contribution of scholars such as John Milton, John Locke and John Stuart Mill. These luminaries believed that people were capable of taking intelligent decisions if an environment of free expression existed. In principle, this theory operates to present the truth and nurture the pluralism of voices. It is impossible to achieve this if an authority outside itself controls it. Down the years, innumerable new ideas were grafted on to early press libertarianism.

The Communist Theory: This started developing with the rise of communism in the early nineteenth century. The Father of Communism, Karl Marx, borrowing from the ideas of German philosopher Georg Wilhelm Friedrich Hegel, stated that the media in communist societies was to operate essentially to perpetuate and expand the socialist political system. The transmission of social policy was the main justification for the existence of a communist media system. According to this theory, the media is a weapon in the hands of the government. The media is owned and run by the state and operates under the aegis of the communist party. Constructive criticism of failed policies is permitted but criticism of basic ideology is forbidden. The theory is also based on the premise that the masses are too fickle, ignorant and unconcerned with the government to be entrusted with governmental responsibilities. Hence, the media has no role with regard to airing too much information about governmental activities. The media has to collaborate with state and party to achieve the welfare of the common people.

The Social Responsibility Theory: The roots of this theory can be traced back to mid-twentieth century America and linked with the libertarian theory, but goes beyond it. This theory lays emphasis on the press's responsibility towards society, rather than on the freedom of the press. It is considered at a level higher than libertarianism—a sort of intellectual evolutionary trip from the discredited, old libertarianism to a perfected libertarianism, where things are forced to work as they really should have under the libertarian theory. The theorists who worked on this stated that they were libertarians, but socially responsible ones, in contrast to the other libertarians. This theory has been drawn largely from a Hutchins Commission report published in 1947.

Discussion: Media in the information age context

Media and media contexts have been defined and redefined many a time, but with the coming of the information age, the media and media contexts are being seen more closely due to their large spread and impact. Modernity, in which the emergence of the mass media has been a dominant player, has contributed to bringing about a sea change in information access and reach. The media, according to many scholars, has played a significant role in the making of modernization, be it the rise of nationalism, individualism, objectivism, democratization, secularization or urbanization. The mass media is an inextricable part of modern society. Information now reaches an audience, to put it proverbially, at the speed of thought. The Internet has indeed made the world flat, cutting across the boundaries of geography, time, caste, colour and creed. There is no gainsaying that without the media, society would not be able to conduct its affairs effectively. Today, almost every aspect of human life is somehow connected to the media. To say that today every individual, more or less, is a media consumer would not be an exaggeration. Some analysts have calculated that, soon, there will be more mobile phones than human beings on this planet.

In the Indian context, the past three decades have seen the Westernization of election campaigns by two major players—the Congress and the Bharatiya Janata Party (BJP). These mainstream political parties, both in national and state elections, spend millions of rupees on paid media campaigns. The mass media, especially via news channels, newspapers and the online media, has become an intrinsic part of the election apparatus. The Election Commission of India (ECI), which is in charge of conducting elections, has been seized by the menace of 'paid news' during election times by candidates representing national parties.

The past few elections, both at the centre and the states—especially the sixteenth parliamentary election, with Narendra Modi as the star campaigner of the BJP, and the Delhi election, which brought the Aam Aadmi Party's (AAP's) Arvind Kejriwal to power—used innovative campaigning styles, including crowdsourcing and crowdfunding. Despite a ceiling set on election expenses by the ECI, major players spent hundreds of crores of rupees on election campaigning. There were allegations of corporate funding and foreign funding, but these were not key issues in the media discourse.

Modi's disdain for the media in general was apparent in his rallies and road shows during the sixteenth parliamentary election. Once, he even referred to media writers as 'news traders'. As we shall discuss in the later chapters, the emotion and attitude of Modi towards the average journalist remains unchanged.

Notes

1. McQuail, Denis, *McQuail's Mass Communication Theory*, Sixth Edition, Sage, London, 2010
2. Childs, Harwood L., *Public Opinion: Nature, Formation and Role*, Van Nostrand, Princeton, New Jersey, 1965
3. Lippmann, Walter, *Public Opinion*, Free Press, New York, 1965
4. From the *Congress Quarterly* research papers on presidential elections, US Library of Congress, Washington DC, 1992
5. Altheide, David L., and Snow, Robert P., *Media Worlds in the Postjournalism Era*, Aldine de Gruyter, New York, 1984
6. Lowery, Shearon, *Milestones in Mass Communication Research: Media Effects*, Longman Publishers, USA, 1995, p.400
7. Berelson, Bernard R., Lazarsfeld, Paul F., and McPhee, William N., *Voting: A Study of Opinion Formations in a Presidential Campaign*, University of Chicago Press, Chicago, 1954, p.234
8. Lazarsfeld, Paul F., Berelson, Bernard R., and Gaudet, Hazel, *The People's Choice: How the Voter Makes Up His Mind in a Presidential Campaign*, Columbia University Press, 1948
9. Elihu, Katz, "The Two-Step Flow of Communication: An Up-To-Date Report on an Hypothesis", *Public Opinion Quarterly*, Chicago, 1957, Vol.21, pp.61–78
10. Klapper, Joseph, *The Effects of Mass Media*, Bureau of Applied Social Research, Columbia University, New York, Vol.IV, No.52, pp.11–25
11. Bennett, W. Lance, and Iyengar, Shanto, "A New Era of Minimal Effects? The Changing Foundations of Political Communication", Journal of Communication, 2008, Vol.58, No.1, p.707

12. Vavreck, Lynn, "Voter Uncertainty and Candidate Contact: New Influences on Voting Behavior", *Communication in U.S. Elections: New Agendas*, eds Hart, Roderick P., and Shaw, Daron R., Rowman and Littlefield Publishers, Lanham, pp.92–94
13. McCombs, M., and Reynolds, A., "News Influence on Our Pictures of the World", *Media Effects: Advances in Theory and Research*, eds Bryant, Jennings, and Oliver, Mary Beth, Routledge, 2002
14. Cohen, Bernard C., *The Press and Foreign Policy*, Harcourt, New York, 1963
15. McCombs, M., "A Look at Agenda-Setting: Past, Present and Future", Journalism Studies, 2005, Vol.6, No.4, pp.543–557
16. Harrop, Martin, "Voting and the Electorate", *Developments in British Politics 2*, Drucker, Henry, MacMillan, 1983
17. Haselmayer, Martin, Wagner, Markus, and Meyer, Thomas M., "Partisan Bias in Message Selection: Media Gatekeeping of Party Press Releases", *Political Communication*, Vol.34, Issue 3
18. Ibid

2

MEDIA IN INDIA: IMPERATIVES FOR ELECTION CAMPAIGNING

> 'The advancement and diffusion of knowledge is the only guardian of true liberty.'
>
> —JAMES MADISON

The past two decades in India have been quite defining in terms of the reach and accessibility of the media. With viewership growing every day, television has the largest reach and access in India. The newspapers have also been doing better with the rise in literacy. India is probably the only country in the world that has constantly witnessed an upsurge in newspaper readership and circulation. The radio, once seen as a great grass-roots medium, however, is fast losing ground due to various reasons. While FM has gained popularity in urban India, community radio, though still at a nascent stage, holds great promise in connecting with local communities and articulating the voices and concerns of the people. With over a billion mobile handsets with access to air waves, the radio has the potential to become as popular as the transistor used to be many decades ago. As per the Telecom Regulatory Authority of India (TRAI), the total number of Internet subscribers increased from 391.5 million at the end of

December 2016 to 445.96 million at the end of December 2017, with a yearly growth rate of 13.91 per cent.[1] Thanks to Internet access via mobile phones, the use of digital media is gaining ground, as more and more youth across the rural and urban spectra are being connected through the Internet.

India has been a repository of myriad forms of folk media, and despite the popularity of mass media, traditional media has lost neither its relevance nor usage, especially among grass-roots communities. Recent research studies reflect that interpersonal communication at the grass-roots level has better impact than the mass media in the decision-making process of voters.

Political parties, and central and state governments in India use the mass media vigorously to reach out to their various constituencies. A lot of credit must go to the very vibrant media in India, which has reached out to millions of Indians via dozens of languages and scores of dialects. Dependence on the media is a kind of a requisite for political parties, especially months ahead of parliamentary and state assembly elections. Parties use both paid-for (advertising) and unpaid-for (public relations [PR]) coverage in the media. There is a general belief that what appears in the editorial and reportage columns has more credibility than what appears as advertisements. This belief has resulted in candidates and parties clamouring for 'third-party endorsement', as it is called in PR parlance, leading to the malpractice of 'paid media' coverage. Media critics have openly spoken about media houses blatantly using printed tariff cards to this effect. In a report, Paranjoy Guha Thakurta and Kalimekolan Sreenivas Reddy, members of the Press Council of India (PCI) committee, said of paid news:

> The entire operation is clandestine. This malpractice has become widespread and now cuts across newspapers and television channels, small and large, in different languages and located in various parts of the country. What is worse,

these illegal operations have become 'organized' and involve advertising agencies and public relations firms, besides journalists, managers and owners of media companies. Marketing executives use the services of journalists—willingly or otherwise—to gain access to political personalities. So-called 'rate cards' or 'packages' are distributed that often include 'rates' for publication of 'news' items that not merely praise particular candidates but also criticize their political opponents. Candidates who do not go along with such 'extortionist' practices on the part of media organizations are denied coverage.[2]

There is no gainsaying the fact that money power has the potential to impact election outcome. In a prime-time bulletin of news channel Times Now, media activist and commentator Jayaprakash Narayan said that putting together parliamentary, assembly and other elections, political parties spend approximately ₹1,00,000 crore of unaccounted money on campaigning, including on mass media publicity gimmicks.[3]

Let us now look at the media bandwidth in India and the changing trends that reflect the state of interdependence of politics and the media.

Newspaper trends

As per the Registrar of Newspapers for India (RNI) report, the total number of registered publications as of 31 March 2017 stood at 1,14,820, including 16,993 in the newspaper category and 97,827 in the periodical category.[4]

Uttar Pradesh (UP) tops the list, with more than 16,000 registrations, followed by Maharashtra, with more than 14,000. Ten states, including Delhi, Madhya Pradesh, Andhra Pradesh and Rajasthan, have more than 5,000 registered newspapers/

periodicals. Eighteen states and Union Territories have less than 1,000 registrations each, as shown in the chart below:[5]

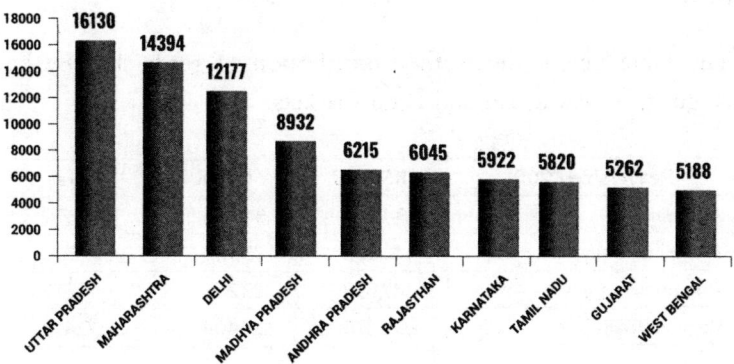

States with more than 5000 registrations

Reach of the print media

As per the latest FICCI-KPMG-Indian Media and Entertainment Industry Report 2016, the circulation of English print publications increased by 5.2 per cent in 2015, whereas the circulation of Hindi and vernacular print publications increased by 11.7 per cent and 8 per cent, respectively. The rise in newspaper readership in India is being propelled by the increase in the number of Hindi and vernacular publications, as existing publications are launching new editions and new publications are entering the media space.

As per the Indian Readership Survey (IRS) 2017, there was a huge surge in newspaper access and readership because of a number of important elections, which included Assam, Goa, Kerala, Manipur, Mizoram, Tamil Nadu, Puducherry and West Bengal in 2016, and UP in the first quarter of 2017. People seemed to be clamouring for information on election news. As the IRS report summed up, 'It is commonly observed that all media consumption in general and print in particular see an increase in such a period, as print is uniquely positioned to cater to the latest national, regional and local political news.'[6]

Print

The table below shows the contribution of readership by key language across urban and rural markets:

Readership ('000)	IRS 2017	Urban	Rural
Any Daily	384,945	84,266	200,679
Any Hindi Daily	176,230	75,730	100,500
Any English Daily	27,535	23,256	4,279
Regional Daily	202,878	102,404	100,474

Source: IRS 2017

As per the IRS data, the higher contribution of Hindi and regional publications is corroborated by the increase in coverage of Hindi and vernacular publications—by means of adding new editions and entering newer markets.

Television

The table below reflects television viewership across population strata:

	All India	>5 lakh towns	<5 lakh towns	Rural
TV Viewership ('000)	782,497	164,127	155,730	462,640

Source: IRS 2017

As is evident from the figures above, rural India is the key contributor to TV viewership: One in two households owns a TV in rural India.

Radio

The table below reflects radio listenership across popular strata:

	All India	>5 lakh towns	<5 lakh towns	Rural
Radio Listenership ('000)	202,733	67,066	34,185	101,482

Source: IRS 2017

Radio, as per IRS data, has 20.27 crore listeners at the all-India level, which is propelled largely by the Phase III implementation of radio station expansion. Large towns, as well as rural India, according to the survey, are key contributors to radio listenership.

Symptoms of the problem

It is not uncommon to hear that news, in general, is becoming highly opinionated and fails to inform and educate, a function traditionally attributed to it. The newspapers across the spectrum do not reflect the plurality of views. Society is often misrepresented. One finds more stereotypes than nuances in news. While it is common knowledge that advertising controls time and space in the media, it is considered less damaging than the surreptitiously organized 'paid news'.

In the case of advertising, the readers know that it is a paid-for space, so there could be exaggerated claims, but when journalists double as paid writers, it certainly is hoodwinking the unsuspecting reader. The blurring lines between advertisements, advertorials and news have been a cause for concern. It is not out of place to mention Medianet, an initiative by the largest circulating English newspaper, which charges money for personal and corporate news published on certain pages. Private equities between media houses and companies is yet another issue of contention that has been discussed and debated on various forums. The PCI has issued guidelines instructing media companies to be transparent in reflecting information on their private treaties publicly, but to no avail. The annexure to the chapter reflects the notice from the Securities and Exchange Board of India (SEBI) to media companies on PCI guidelines.

It is common knowledge that a handful of interests control the media in India. The independence of editors, so far a hallmark of newspapers, has become a thing of the past. Independent voices are fading. The biases of most journalists are clear to even first-time readers/viewers. Public concerns and issues do not seem to be part of any serious political, social, economic or policy debate in the media.

Amid all this chaos, the redeeming factor, however, is that some newspapers have oriented themselves to the requirements of the readers—their interface with readers is now more defined than ever before. Citizen journalists have been writing for some newspapers, while others have readers' editors and ombudsmen to ensure that news items are published with fairness and propriety. With a well-laid-out professional code of ethics propounded by media associations, it is hoped that more accountability will be demanded of media writers in future, in the interest of safeguarding the profession's credibility.

Ownership patterns in print media

There have been changing ownership patterns in the Indian print media over the past six decades. Today, there are all kinds of vested interests in newspapers—including political, religious, corporate and global. This issue has been debated in detail in the chapter "Media Objectivity: Reality or Myth?" There has been increasing corporatization of the media and growing oligopolistic trends. The bigger newspapers, with their large cache of resources and strategies, garner maximum ad revenue, leaving the smaller newspapers struggling for recognition. The government has opened up the news sector to foreign direct investment (FDI). Earlier, FDI was allowed only up to 26 per cent. In the non-news sector too, the limit is now 100 per cent from the previous limit of 74 per cent.

Preserving press freedom

Freedom of speech and expression is guaranteed by the Indian Constitution, but it has not always been easy for the Indian media. The declaration of Emergency in 1975 by former prime minister Indira Gandhi saw for the first time the state's repression of the media through censorship. While many buckled under pressure, some bold newspapers, such as *The Indian Express* and *The Statesman*, carried blank editorials and stories, rather than censored ones on many occasions.

The PCI was established under an act of the Parliament for 'preserving the freedom of the press' and 'maintaining and improving the standards of newspapers and news agencies in India'. The chairman of the PCI, a retired judge of the Supreme Court of India, has a council of twenty-eight members—twenty representing the newspapers industry, five from the Parliament (three nominated by the speaker of Lok Sabha and two by the chairman of Rajya Sabha) and the remaining three from the Sahitya Akademi, the Bar Council of India and the University Grants Commission. The council has its own revenue source—it collects a levy from registered newspapers and news agencies—and gets grant-in-aid from the government for performing its functions.

The PCI discharges its duties primarily through adjudications or complaints it receives, either against the press for violation of the journalistic code or by the press for interference with its freedom. The council is also empowered to make such observations as it may deem fit in respect of the conduct of any authority, including the government, for interfering with the freedom of the press. The decisions of the council are final and cannot be challenged in any court of law. However, despite its many rulings, the newspaper industry in general does not take them seriously.

Television in India

Indian television has witnessed phenomenal growth, especially in the past two decades or so. No one would have imagined in 1959, when television was launched in Delhi with the transmission of educational and developmental programmes on an experimental basis, that it would see such exponential growth. There are over 800 channels that include more than 400 news and business channels that broadcast 24x7.

According to the FICCI-KPMG-Indian Media and Entertainment Industry Report 2016, India is the second-largest television market in the world, reaching out to 175 million households in 2015, with a penetration of 62 per cent. The number of Cable & Satellite (C&S) subscribers is estimated to have reached 160 million. Excluding Doordarshan (DD) Free Dish, the number of paid C&S subscribers is estimated to have been 145 million in 2015, implying a paid C&S penetration of 83 per cent.

News channels don't restrict themselves to news programmes alone, but have a variety of fare on offer, which include entertainment programmes, studio-based programmes and vox pop on myriad issues.

The total reach of all the news channels in India put together is less than two digits, but the viewership surges when there is a crisis situation, giving the news channels immense reach and credibility.

One thing that is prevalent, at least among the mainstream English and Hindi channels, is the studio-based approach to news. It is disheartening to see that, on every issue, only the spokespersons of various parties are invited. Field reporting and voices from the grass roots seem to have become a thing of the past. The screen is split into eight to ten windows represented by the same people day after day, week after week, who seem to have expertise on everything under the sun. The trivialization of public discourse is too obvious to escape notice. As for the invitees, they seem to be in demand in all the competitive channels, and it is not uncommon to see some of them demanding an 'early hearing', so that they can reach other studios.

News is packaged with publicity paraphernalia such as graphics, infographics, the flashing of the profiles of anchors, split screens, simultaneous vox pop via audio and, not to forget, the new trend of using the graphic of flames for a discussion too 'hot' to handle.

With so much drama, the political parties and candidates clamour for even a minute of fame during election time. The television channels are happy to oblige, albeit, as mentioned earlier, probably for a price.

Radio in India

The All India Radio (AIR) is said to be one of the largest broadcasting networks in the world. At the time of India's independence in 1947, the AIR had six radio stations and eighteen transmitters, which covered only 11 per cent of the population. This has increased to 233 stations and 375 transmitters reaching 99.6 per cent of the population and 91.82 per cent area of the country.[7] The news-service division broadcasts 647 news bulletins every day for a cumulative period of 56 hours in 90 languages and dialects via home, regional, external and direct-to-home (DTH) services. Besides, 314 news bulletins are also aired on an hourly basis via FM Rainbow and other frequency channels from 41 AIR stations. However, thanks to unnecessary government control, despite an investment that runs into billions of rupees on manpower, programming, broadcasting and infrastructure, the reach is going down miserably. FM radio stations are gaining some ground, but they are not allowed to broadcast news. This seems unreasonable in a country that has hundreds of television channels beaming news 24x7. What difference radio news will make is something only the mandarins in the Information & Broadcasting (I&B) Ministry can explain.

With a great grass-roots connect, radio, which can also be accessed from mobile phones, can reach every nook and cranny of the country. Many states have also used it befittingly during disasters.

Digital media in India

The Internet has achieved what all other forms of the media put together could not. The Internet, in a short span, has connected communities in real time, and made governments and those occupying public offices more alert and responsive. Social media platforms have empowered the common man, who is now expressing joy, sorrow and angst via these, along with seeking accountability from companies, public institutions and the government. This probably is the reason why the government has become so active, led by Prime Minister (PM) Narendra Modi, on social media platforms. However, how active the top echelons should be on social media is a debatable issue.

Social media platforms, especially Facebook and Twitter, are used as primary media during elections by political parties and candidates for connecting with the youth. A lot of credit is ascribed to the strategic use of the Internet by the BJP, especially by PM Modi, for leading his party to victory in the sixteenth parliamentary election.

Deconstructing mass media strengths and weaknesses

Each medium has its own strengths, weaknesses and salient features. The media is relevant only when matched carefully with messages and audiences. In the following tables, relative strengths and weaknesses of the various forms of media have been listed.

Print media

Press	
Strengths	**Weaknesses**
Messages received at home in a relaxed atmosphere	Suffers from the literacy barrier
Readers look forward to receiving their newspaper; has shelf value	Low shelf life, as newspapers become stale in a day
The urge to seek news puts the newspaper in a better position to be trusted	Lacks drama and emotion
Reading a newspaper becomes a matter of habit, hence it achieves regular attention value	Demonstration of product features not effective
Has scope for detailed coverage	Overtaken by television in speed
The written word has more credibility	Lacks empathetic readership
Messages carry a sense of urgency	'Bad' news is often considered 'good' news
Can be read at leisure	What is of reader's interest is decided by the newspapers
High on national coverage	Average time devoted to newspaper reading is very low, hence ads don't stand much chance of being seen carefully

Local/regional newspapers	
Strengths	**Weaknesses**
Strong reader loyalty	Low circulation
Local coverage	Vulnerable to biases
Regional flexibility	Generally poor readership data

Magazines

Strengths	Weaknesses
Selective readership	High production cost
High shelf value	Long copy and cancellation dates
Creates a bond and empathy with the readers	Expensive advertising medium
High on style, design and colour	High printing cost

Television

Strengths	Weaknesses
Reaches a wide audience	Expensive for time and production
Sight, sound and colour give it a dramatic character	Bad quality, transmission issues and poor anchors may put viewers off
Larger-than-life images	Heavy viewing can lead to eyesight problems
Achieves viewers' empathy	Tends to make people 'home birds' and asocial
High on credibility	Can adversely and easily influence impressionable minds
Wide choice of channels without any extra cost	Too much airing of sex and violence can have an adverse impact on society
A family medium	Transient messages

Radio

Strengths	Weaknesses
Wide coverage	Suffers from apathetic listeners
High OTS (Opportunity to See) among listeners	Audience intently uses it as 'audio wallpaper'
Advertising inexpensive, as compared to TV and press	TV preferred over radio, if there is a choice
Long broadcasting hours	Speed of broadcast (short lead time)
High impact and immediacy	Not a very interactive medium
If used as a transistor, a mobile medium	Not very innovative

Cinema

Strengths	Weaknesses
Impact of the big screen, with sound, movement and colour	TV has eroded the cinema audience base
Attracts the young crowd	Slow build-up of audience
Theatre-viewing a socializing event	Attendance is low and infrequent
Selective local advertising coverage possible, which can gain immediate impact	Commercials shown either in the beginning or during the interval, when high attendance is not ensured

Outdoor (posters, billboards, hoarding)

Strengths	Weaknesses
High coverage OTS	High printing cost of posters, unless used on a large scale
Large-size billboards project a larger-than-life image	Suffers poor audience research
Sites can be booked flexibly	Bone of contention with environmentalists, as they spoil the landscape
Can create drama with colour and size	Strong winds can damage boards and lead to accidents
Twenty-four-hour projection	With electronic hoardings, short circuits possible in monsoon
Good reminder medium	Only small messages possible
A community medium	Can distract drivers[8]

Internet/digital media

Strengths	Weaknesses
Global networking	Low access
Seamless coverage	Information overload
No hierarchical set-up for access of information	Banner ad recall not very high
High interactivity	Low on research, hence not a favourite medium with media planners
By and large a free-to-access medium	Message spillover to unrequired territories
Instant connectivity	Not a medium to suit all demographic profiles

A storehouse of knowledge	Requires time commitment
Online marketing	

Mobile phones and SMS

Strengths	Weaknesses
A revolutionary communication form	Can become a nuisance if left unchecked
Reach not dependent on location	Intrusion on privacy
Can easily reach the right target audience	A possible health hazard
Permission marketing possible	Can lead to overdependence on this medium
Emotional connotation	A group socialization tool
An all-pervasive medium	Can contribute to creating grapevine and irresponsible messaging

Source: Advertising Management, J. Jethwaney and Shruti Jain, Second Edition, OUP, 2011

Folk media

India has a vibrant folk media culture. The interpersonal mode of communication and instant audience feedback have made folk media the most-sought-after choice by various political parties during election times.

The following table lists out the popular folk media forms in India:

Folk form	Region	Description
Alha	Madhya Pradesh and Uttar Pradesh	Song form: Requires a four-member group—two singers and two instrument players (it is a popular narrative on the heroic deeds of the Alha brothers[9])

Bhopa	Rajasthan	Song and dance form: Team consists of husband, wife and child. The wife and child sing and dance, and the husband plays the instrument
Birha	Eastern Uttar Pradesh	Song form. Requires a team of four to six persons
Burra Katha	Andhra Pradesh	Drama form
Dandiya and Garba	Gujarat	Dance form
Jatra	West Bengal, Odisha	Stylized folk drama, originally of devotional nature, now increasingly used for social awakening
Kabbigaan	West Bengal	A musical arrangement between two teams of skilful artistes, improvising for and against a given message
Kathakali	Kerala	Dance form
Lavaani	Maharashtra	Dance form. Usually performed on romantic songs. Originated during the Peshwa period. It is a ballad on historical and social themes sung by two artistes
Tamasha	Maharashtra	Similar to Nautanki. It is robust, topical, musical and humorous
Burrakatha	Andhra Pradesh	An ingenious folk performance, presented by three artistes with burras, or talking drums (tambura)
Bhavai	Gujarat	A true representation of Gujarat's colours and costumes, well known for improvisation, humour and satire
Longa and Maganyar	Rajasthan	Drama and song form. Requires a team of four, out of whom two are usually tribal
Naca	Madhya Pradesh	Dance and drama form. Requires a five- to six-member team
Nautanki	Uttar Pradesh, Bihar and Haryana	Drama mixed with folk songs. Requires a team of four to ten performers

Puppetry	Northern India	Drama and song form. Makes use of puppets, whether string puppets, glove puppets, shadow puppets or rod puppets
Pabo Ji Ki Pad	Rajasthan	Pad (phad) is a scroll of sequential panels of figures and situations, painted in colour. The stories are scriptural. A curtain is stretched out between two poles, and an earthen lamp illuminates the panel from behind as the narrators sing the stories to the audience
Qawwali	Madhya Pradesh and Uttar Pradesh	Songs adapted from the sher-o-shayari tradition, usually descriptive in nature
Ragini	Haryana	Legends and folklore narrated in song form
Wasilla	Uttar Pradesh	Based on the Rasleela form, which has one male and a few female dancers; based on the shringar rasa
Swang	Haryana and eastern Punjab	Drama-form dialogues interspersed with song; requires a team of five who play the nagara and sing folk tunes to attract crowds
Yakshagana	Karnataka and Tamil Nadu	The southern counterpart of Nautanki
Vellupaattu	Tamil Nadu and Kerala	The 'bow song' is sung by six to eight artistes, plucking on the string of a large bow for keeping rhythm

Source: Communication and Traditional Media, IIMC, 1981

The use of folk songs, ballads, folk tales and riddles has been common in election campaigns. Parties use folk theatre popular in their respective states—such as jatra in West Bengal, Odisha and eastern Bihar; tamasha in Maharashtra; nautanki in UP, Rajasthan and Punjab; bhavai in Gujarat; yakshagana in Karnataka; and therubuttu in Tamil Nadu. Maintaining basic conventions such as stage preliminaries, the use of a sutradhar (narrator), a vidushak (buffoon) and an opening prayer song, folk theatre has achieved quick mass appeal. Folk plays provide valuable insight into the dialect, attire, attitude, humour and wit of the states in which they are staged.

If politics has an agenda, so does the media

Democracy and the media are like Siamese twins, each complementing the other, yet no debate can be conclusive about their true relationship and interdependence. There has always been a love-hate relationship between politics and the media, although some scholars tend to believe that the media and politics cross-fertilize each other, one needing the other for survival.

Both institutions draw their supposed power from the public—politics from the power of the people who elect representatives to political institutions, and the media from the eyeballs it is able to grab through news, entertainment programmes and coverage of events, personalities and ideas. The existence of 'power' in politics is inherent, but in the media, the power is 'assumed' or 'acquired'. In a way, both politics and the media can be said to be 'power institutions'. The engagement of politics with the media and of the media with politics will not go away anytime soon—but equations are redefined from time to time.

Media bias: impact on politics

Stefano DellaVigna and Ethan Kaplan in their insightful paper "The Political Impact of Media Bias" say that 'in a representative system of government, policy outcomes are affected by the political preferences and the beliefs of the voters. The media plays a key role in shaping these preferences and beliefs. It collects, summarizes and frames the information that voters use in their voting decisions.'[10]

It is believed that Lasswell did some of the earliest known political content analysis with magazines. He investigated themes of Nazism in US publications for legal purposes during the Second World War. *Reader's Digest* and *The Saturday Evening Post* were compared to publications allegedly guilty of Nazi propaganda.[11] Quoting from various studies undertaken by various researchers, Lawrence J. Mullen, in his article "An Overview of Political Content Analyses of Magazines"[12], comments that in recent years, strict quantitative description has become less important. Instead, studies using magazine content to support rhetorical arguments[13] show ideological manipulation in the news media[14] or support an argument about how the media portrays individuals—for instance, how magazines depict politicians' wives[15] or how media content and form are inseparable.[16]

The framing theory posits that something is presented to the audience/reader as a 'frame', which, in turn, influences the audience to make a choice. Frames, argue scholars, help in lending meaning to messages. First presented by Canadian-American sociologist Erving Goffman, the framing theory is based on the premise that people interpret what is going on around them through their primary framework. This framework is regarded as primary, as it is taken for granted by the user. Its usefulness as a framework does not depend on other frameworks. Goffman argues that there are two frameworks—natural and social—and both have a role in how an individual will interpret data.[17]

In her masters-level thesis, "Julian Assange: A Content Analysis of Media Framing in Newspapers Around the World", Meylin K. Menjivar Andrade examined through the method of content analysis how the media framed Julian Assange after the Ecuadorian government granted him political asylum at its embassy in London on 16 August 2012. The researcher compared 380 English- and Spanish-language newspaper articles from North America, Europe, Australia/New Zealand, Asia and Latin America to examine regional differences in the way Assange was framed.[18]

Impact of the mass media on the voting behaviour of Indians

There are many factors that affect the voting behaviour of Indian citizens. Mass media stimuli and other forms of election-campaign work at both subtle and manifest levels in shaping the decision-making process. In the context of an average Indian voter, there is a belief that he/she is politically savvy and understands the value of his/her vote, notwithstanding the power of caste, money and muscle.

Whether the media enhances or hinders the democratic process in an election is a question that deserves an equally serious debate. Political Science professor Zoya Hasan in the news article "Manufacturing Dissent: The Media and the 2014 Indian Election" commented that when the campaign for the sixteenth parliamentary election was at its peak and the prime ministerial candidate Narendra Modi was on his whirlwind campaigning spree, a few media houses and editors had created a discourse around him, dubbing the ten years of the United Progressive Alliance (UPA) government a 'wasted decade' and the last sixty years of the Indian republic insignificant in terms of development and progress, thus exhorting voters to give sixty months to Modi against the last sixty years to prove himself. To quote her, 'media in India does not merely report, it is a player in the Indian politics and elections'.[19]

Journalist Sandeep Bhushan, in his analytical article in *The Caravan* "How the Television News Industry Scripted the Indian Elections", commented that it was for history to judge how myriad languages and multiple dialects across more than 400 news channels throughout the length and breadth of India evolved a discourse around a person. To quote Bhushan, 'beyond obvious and hidden pressures that have driven television news, the real rupture in narrative has been a sea change in the very grammar of television content. ... [T]he trends in television coverage [that] have emerged in the course of these elections—all uniformly designed to strengthen the studio and the anchor, instead of empowering the reporter.'[20]

If one looks at prime-time news bulletins across mainstream news channels in India, they all look the same. The news becomes what a group of invited guests talk about, with the anchor making no bones about the positioning he has on the issue under discussion. 'The irony is that all networks routinely talk about "deepening democracy" within the rarefied confines of the studio,' comments Bhushan. 'But they seldom permit the creation of news content that will reflect the country's unfolding diversity, especially visible during election time.'[21]

The Harvard Kennedy School student publication carried an interesting analysis of the Indian media in its 18 August 2015 issue. Titled "Indian Media: Crisis in the Fourth Estate", it said,

> Indian media is currently in a state of pliable crisis, susceptible to the external influences of various branches of government and business. This is a grave policy issue. Media guards democracy; paid news and pliable journalism put public opinion at the mercy of money and advertisers. To be clear, Modi has not had this effect directly on the media—it was subpar in its ethical standards long before Modi entered the scene, and paid news at election time was reported to be a grave problem even in the election of 2009. It is the combination of a leader with little tolerance for dissent and a self-censoring journalism industry that makes the current scenario uniquely worrying.[22]

In a doctoral thesis to gauge the impact of political communication on the voting behaviour of people in three southern Indian states—Karnataka, Kerala and Tamil Nadu—it was found that different campaign strategies had different impacts on voting behaviour. While political rallies, meetings, jathas and campaign speeches had the maximum impact on voting behaviour in Karnataka, door-to-door campaigning had the maximum impact in Kerala, whereas discussion and debate through television channels had the maximum impact in Tamil Nadu. Party newspapers had almost equal impact on the voting behaviour in Karnataka and Kerala; election manifestos had almost similar impacts in Kerala and Tamil Nadu, but not so much in Karnataka. Street plays as a campaign strategy had more impact on the voters in Karnataka than in Kerala and Tamil Nadu.[23]

It is interesting how the mass media was second to interpersonal communication in impacting voting behaviour in the three states mentioned above.

A study of the impact of social media on the voting behaviour of Indians during the sixteenth parliamentary election, by Aindrila Biswas, Nikhil Ingle and Mousumi Roy, brings to attention some interesting findings and insights. Traditional media channels such as television and print leveraged social media conversations and discussions to share real-time news and views around political parties. Online banner ads and other forms of advertising had a significant impact on young voters, especially students, which not only influenced them but also helped in shaping their behaviour, the study found. It was discovered that conversation on social media forums influenced female voters more than their male counterparts, which indirectly affected their decision to vote. Women followed the political candidate on Twitter and Facebook, and actively engaged in political discussion by expressing their views and opinions. It was inferred that people were more likely to favour or vote for that party which was most digitally interactive on social media. It was also found that the decisions of those who were highly active on social media were likely to be affected by what they read on a particular politician.[24]

An insightful content analysis of four English newspapers by a research team to gauge their political orientation during the sixteenth parliamentary election found that despite the Indian press being free from state regulations in India, there was overt bias in favour of one party. The newspapers selected were *Hindustan Times*, *The Times of India*, *The Hindu* and *The Telegraph*. The research was conducted from 21 January to 12 May 2014. "India 2014: Press Trend as a Predictor of Election Outcome" by Francis P. Barclay et al is significant in many ways. Scientific methods of content analysis that looked at both the quantitative and the qualitative aspects of coverage showed that despite varying political orientations of these four newspapers, the BJP received highly favourable coverage across the board. The study checked for shifts in the endorsement during the period of the study and found that the political orientation of all the four newspapers had changed significantly during the period of research.[25]

A few questions emerge. To what could this favourable coverage be attributed? Was it the publicity apparatus mounted by the party? Was it Modi's gift of the gab? Was it the anti-incumbency factor against the ruling Congress? Or was it the creation of the perception of a 'non-performing' government, the intangible expression of 'the policy paralysis' that gained ground, and the stories about the alleged multiple scams? The media had been incessantly writing on these issues for a long time, so to write in favour of the Congress or to look closely at its achievements did not seem to be a possibility around that time. On the part of the Congress, its leaders gave the impression of defeat, even before giving the Opposition a fight. The BJP obviously was the beneficiary of media favouritism.

But looking at a time when the BJP had completed two years in office, the discourse seemed to have gone sour. The growing negative narrative on 'intolerance', the beef controversy, the aftermath of Dalit student Rohith Vemula's suicide that brought together youth from across campuses and the Jawaharlal Nehru

University (JNU) sedition story did not augur well for the person who had done something impossible for the party just two years back. Then came demonetization in November 2016, the withdrawal of the high-denomination currency notes with the aim to check black money. Despite the hardships faced by the general public, the high-decibel rhetoric by most of the Opposition parties, their march to the President's House and an almost riot-like situation, which seemed to be endorsed by India's highest court, the average Indian showed unparalleled resilience and patience. While the PM kept saying in his speeches outside the Parliament that he was not given the chance to speak in Parliament, and the Opposition—especially Rahul Gandhi, then Congress vice president—kept challenging him to speak in Parliament, the common man waited for days, weeks and sometimes even over a month to deposit or withdraw money from his own bank account! The analysts thought this could be a big embarrassment for the PM and prove to be his nemesis, but it did not seem so, as the PM didn't leave any stone unturned in talking about his intentions behind demonetization at his rallies in UP—a state that was to go to the polls in a few months, in early 2017.

Author Chetan Bhagat, in an opinionated article, commented that this was because of the three Is—intention, initiative and idea—which people seemed to be impressed with, despite the fact that the quantum of black money that was expected to be rounded up at the end of demonetization was not unearthed.[26]

Politics is a game of chess, dependent on many variables. Similarly, public opinion formation depends on many factors, the media being only one of the players that provide the stimulus. What really works for one but against the other in an election is a moot point.

Annexure

SEBI updates

SEBI protects the interests of investors in securities and promotes the development of the securities market through appropriate regulation. This blog contains 'what's new' with SEBI and the securities market in India.

Tuesday, 31 August 2010

PR No.200/2010

Mandatory disclosures by the media of its stake in the corporate sector

SEBI had taken up with Press Council of India its concerns on the practice of many media groups entering into agreements, such as 'private treaties', with companies. Typically, such arrangements are with companies which are listed or which propose to come out with public offerings. These, in general, entail a company giving stake in it (shares, warrants, bonds, etc.) in return for media coverage through advertisements, news reports, advertorials, etc., in print or electronic media. It was felt that such agreements may give rise to a conflict of interest and may, therefore, result in dilution of the independence of press. This may consequently compromise the nature, quality and content of the news/editorials relating to such companies. Needless to say, biased and motivated dissemination of information, guided by commercial considerations, can potentially mislead investors in the securities market. Such journalism would not be in the interest of the securities market. SEBI, given its legal mandate to protect the interest of investors, felt that such brand-building strategies of media groups, without appropriate and adequate disclosures, may not be in the interest of investors and financial markets. There are the prescribed norms of journalistic conduct that require journalists to disclose any interest that they may have in the company about which they are reporting. However, there are no equivalent requirements in the case of media companies holding a stake in the company being reported or covered.

The Press Council of India has informed SEBI that in its meeting held on 22 February 2010 in New Delhi, it has accepted the following suggestions of SEBI and has mandated the following:

1) Disclosures regarding stake held by the media company should be made in the news report/ article/editorial in newspapers/television relating to the company in which the media group holds such stake.
2) Disclosure on the percentage of stake held by media groups in various companies under such 'Private Treaties' on the website of media groups should be made.
3) Any other disclosures related to such agreements, such as any nominee of the media group on the Board of Directors of the company, any management control or other details which may be required to be disclosed and which may be a potential conflict of interest for the media group, should also be mandatorily disclosed.

The copy of the press release sent to SEBI by Press Council of India in the matter is enclosed.

The above is for information and necessary compliance by all concerned.

Mumbai
27 August 2010

Notes

1. https://www.trai.gov.in/sites/default/files/YPIRReport04052018.pdf.
2. Thakurta, Paranjoy G., and Reddy, Kalimekolan S., "Paid News: How Corruption in the Indian Media Undermines Democracy", 1 April 2010
www.indiatogether.org/uploads/document/document_upload/2146/PCIsc-intro.pdf
3. 10 p.m. bulletin by Arnab Goswami, Times Now, 14 November 2016
4. In response to Unstarred Question No.7,019, answered on 8 May 2015 in the Lok Sabha, Ministry of Information & Broadcasting and Directorate of Advertising and Visual Publicity (DAVP), Government of India
https://factly.in/indian-newspapers-more-than-one-lakh-newspapers-periodicals-registered-in-the-country/
5. Dubbudu, Rakesh, "More Than a Lakh Newspapers & Periodicals Are Registered in the Country", Factly.in, 28 May 2015
https://factly.in/indian-newspapers-more-than-one-lakh-newspapers-periodicals-registered-in-the-country/
6. http://mruc.net/uploads/posts/2b17d38a6cf860f0aabf1695c48b27ca.pdf
7. http://allindiaradio.gov.in/Default.aspx
8. The Supreme Court ordered the removal of roadside hoardings in Delhi in its ruling in November 1997. On 24 November, the Municipal Corporation of Delhi issued a notice of forty-eight hours to advertisers to remove unauthorized hoardings or face seizure. The Supreme Court's order came in the wake of increasing instances of road accidents, especially after one of the worst bus accidents in history, in which twenty-eight schoolchildren died when the driver plunged the bus into the Yamuna river on 17 November 1997. Quoting an advertiser, *The Times of India* in its issue of 23 November, wrote, 'Accidents take place because drivers drive rashly and not because they get distracted by hoardings.' Also see *Express Newsline*

of *The Indian Express*, 24 November 1997.
9. It consists of a number of ballads describing the brave acts of two twelfth-century Banaphar Rajput heroes, Alha and Udai, two generals working for King Paramardi-Deva (Parmal) of Mahoba (1163–1202 CE) against the attacker Prithviraj (1149–1192 CE) of Delhi. Hiltebeitel, Alf, *Rethinking India's Oral and Classical Epics: Draupadi Among Rajputs, Muslims, and Dalits*, University of Chicago Press, 2009, p.163
10. DellaVigna, Stefano, and Kaplan, Ethan, "The Political Impact of Media Bias", Information and Public Choice, World Bank Publications http://eml.berkeley.edu/~sdellavi/wp/mediabiaswb07-06-25.pdf
11. Hofstetter, Richard C., "Content Analysis", *Handbook of Political Communication*, eds Nimmo, Dan D., and Sanders, Keith R., Sage, Beverly Hills, 1981, pp.529–560
12. Mullen, Lawrence J., "An Overview of Political Content Analyses of Magazines", The Electronic Journal of Communication, 1994 http://www.cios.org/EJCPUBLIC/004/2/004219.html
13. Hart, Roderick P., Smith-Howell, Deborah, and Llewellyn, John, "The Mindscape of the Presidency: Time Magazine, 1945-1985", *Journal of Communication*, 1991, Vol.41, No.3, pp.6–25
14. Herman, Edward S., and Chomsky, Noam, *Manufacturing Consent: The Political Economy of the Mass Media*, Pantheon Books, New York, 1988
15. Nimmo, Dan, and Combs, James E., "Political Celebrity in Popular Magazines", *Mediated Political Realities*, Longman, New York, 1983, pp.92–104
16. Altheide, David L., and Snow, Robert P., *Media Logic: A Sage Library Research Book #89*, Sage, Beverly Hills, 1979
17. Goffman, Erving, *Frame Analysis: An Essay on the Organization of Experience*, Harper & Row, New York, 1974
18. Andrade, Meylin K.M., "Julian Assange: A Content Analysis of Media Framing in Newspapers Around the World", East Tennessee State University, 2013
http://dc.etsu.edu/cgi/viewcontent.cgi?article=2336&context=etd

19. Hasan, Zoya, "Manufacturing Dissent: The Media and the 2014 Indian Election", The Hindu Centre for Politics and Public Policy, 2 April 2014
https://www.thehinducentre.com/verdict/commentary/article5843621.ece
20. Bhushan, Sandeep, "How the Television News Industry Scripted the Indian Elections", *The Caravan*, 15 May 2014
http://www.caravanmagazine.in/vantage/television-scripted
21. Ibid
22. Khan, Uzra, "Indian Media: Crisis in the Fourth Estate", Kennedy School Review, 2016 Issue, 18 August 2015
http://ksr.hkspublications.org/2015/08/18/indian-media-crisis-in-the-fourth-estate/
23. Jacob, Nirmal, "The Impact of Political Communication On Voting Behaviour: A Comparative Study In Karnataka, Kerala & Tamil Nadu", University of Mysore, 2010
http://shodhganga.inflibnet.ac.in/bitstream/10603/15902/16/16_synopsis.pdf
24. Biswas, Aindrila, Ingle, Nikhil, and Roy, Mousumi, "Influence of Social Media on Voting Behavior", *Journal of Power, Politics & Governance*, June 2014, Vol.2, No.2, pp.127–155
25. Barclay, Francis P., Pichandy, C., Venkat, Anusha, and Sudhakaran, Sreedevi, "India 2014: Press Trend as a Predictor of Election Outcome", New Directions in Media, eds Islam, K.M. Baharul, and Roy, Nandita, Bloomsbury Publishing India
https://www.academia.edu/22280685/India_2014_Press_trend_as_a_predictor_of_election_outcome
26. Bhagat, Chetan, "The Three New I's of Indian Politics", *The Times of India*, 24 December 2016, p.22

3

MEDIA OBJECTIVITY: REALITY OR MYTH?

> 'An unexamined life is a life of no account.'
> —SOCRATES

Is the media objective? Is the media a crusade or just a job like any other or a business proposition? What role does the media play in society and is it fulfilling that role? What are the expectations of various stakeholders, especially citizens, from the media? Questions such as these defy any substantive answers but generate a lot of heat in academic circles, among opinion makers and the concerned citizenry. Journalism, ideally, is supposed to follow the cardinal principle that facts are sacrosanct and comment is free. However, in reality, it may not always be practical. Journalistic values, though supposedly neutral, introduce an element of 'random partisanship' to the issue under discussion, which coincidentally works to the advantage of one at the cost of the other.

Media content, before it reaches the audience, goes through a number of decisions, which include the kind of stories to be done, how much space should be allotted to them, what positions they should occupy and what slant should be given to them, depending on the general position of the paper or the channel. These conditions, according to media analysts, make the media partisan. There is a growing feeling that there are no objective lessons to follow, but only conventions.

Many scholars such as Brants, Franklin, and Sparks & Tulloch have referred to the new hybrid formats that 'mix political information and entertainment, such as infotainment, politainment, political talk shows and reality television' in the media content to make it less objective.[1] Political reporting is increasingly 'characterized by tabloidization. No longer are human-interest stories, sensationalism and colloquial language confined to the tabloid press. The quality press and public service news programmes are employing similar formats to attract new audiences or at least to prevent a further erosion of circulation rates,' lament the authors.[2]

Edward S. Herman and Noam Chomsky in their much-celebrated book *Manufacturing Consent: The Political Economy of the Mass Media*, comment that the media, in order to appear objective, does not mind giving weight to 'official sources' to appear accurate. They also argue that 'partly to maintain the image of objectivity, but also to protect themselves from criticisms of bias and the threat of libel suits, they need material that can be portrayed as presumptively accurate'.[3]

Expanding on their propaganda model, Herman and Chomsky argue that the media in general serves and propagandizes on behalf of the powerful societal interest that controls and finances them. This, they say, is done very smartly, by the 'selection of right-thinking personnel and the editors and working journalists' internalization of priorities and definitions of news-worthiness that conforms to the Institution's policy'.[4]

In 1973, Leon Sigal, commenting on the press, wrote, 'Most news is not what has happened, but what someone says has happened', referring to the information flow from various sources, the government and other entities.[5] All the arguments, in a way, posit that 'news' has the inherent character of being created. In a way, 'post-truth', the *Oxford Dictionary*'s Word of the Year in 2016, defines most of the news media content today, especially in the context of election campaigning.[6] Political commentators have identified post-truth politics as ascendant in Russian, Chinese, American, Australian, British, Indian, Japanese and Turkish politics, as well as in other areas of debate, driven by a combination of the 24-hour news cycle, a false balance in news reporting and the increasing ubiquity of social media.[7]

Quoting political scientist Lance Bennet, Thomas E. Patterson, in his book *Informing the News: The Need for Knowledge-Based Journalism*, comments that power, rather than truthfulness, is the operative standard of 'he said, she said' reporting. Patterson strongly canvasses for 'knowledge-based journalism', which, in his view, seems to be a rarity.[8]

While canvassing for the sixteenth parliamentary election, Modi, the then BJP PM-designate, coined a new term, 'news traders', for journalists, questioning the intent and honesty of scribes. It was, in a way, belittling the role of journalists by alluding to their bias in news stories. TV news anchor and journalist Rajdeep Sardesai in a news column in *Mint*, "Modi and Me", commented, 'If Mr Modi could target professional journalists as "news traders", then perhaps his admirers felt they had the license to do the same. The anonymity of social media provided some of them fresh ammunition to abuse...'[9]

Sardesai, who was in the US to cover Modi's maiden visit to the country in September 2014 after becoming PM, incidentally faced a violent mob that roughed him up at Madison Square for being critical of Modi. Here is what *The Financial Express* reported on the incident:

> Leading TV anchor Rajdeep Sardesai was today roughed up apparently by pro-Modi supporters outside the Madison Square Garden, shortly before Prime Minister Narendra

Modi's address. The news created quite a buzz on social networking site Twitter after @JFK_America posted, 'Mob of people attacking an Indian journalist for being critical of Narendra Modi in the past. Accused of being a traitor.' Rajdeep Sardesai, who quit as the editor-in-chief of IBN 18 Network in July, tweeted, 'Great crowd at Madison square garden! except [sic] a few idiots who still believe abuse is a way of proving their machismo!' He added, 'Glad we caught the idiots on cam. Only way to shame the mob is to show them.' Sardesai also posted, 'Great publicity for my book. All those who took selfies have promised to buy it.'[10]

Despite almost 90 per cent of the media houses openly writing off US President Donald Trump and expressing their disdain of him in the 2016 presidential campaign, he made it to the presidency, putting all prognosis by the media and researchers to rest. Whether Trump is the right choice is besides the point; that an overwhelming chunk of the media went wrong puts a serious question mark on the capability of the US media in understanding and assimilating the pulse of the nation and this is a serious issue that needs empirical research on the inherent bias of the media in reporting ground reality. James Hohmann's comment in his story in *The Washington Post* puts it succinctly, 'President-elect Donald Trump was right all along. He had the silent majority. The media, pollsters and Republican elites never saw it—even though it was right in front of them the whole time.'[11] The media arithmetic also went for a toss in India in the March 2017 UP Assembly election, where media houses wrote about '*kante ki takkar*' (close fight) between the BJP and the Samajwadi Party (SP)-Congress. Former adman and social commentator Santosh Desai said that while the media went wrong in predicting the outcome, as soon as the results were announced, they all became experts on why it had happened. To quote him,

In all fairness, the job of a commentator in today's time is to provide instant analysis. Ideally, one should take time to look at data and arrive at a hypothesis that helps explain what happened, but the nature of the news cycle does not allow that. But, perhaps, the certitude could be tempered and some humility be in evidence. If we were so wrong about what was going to happen, how are we so sure about why it happened? ... Given the low credibility that the media enjoys today, these are questions that need some thought.[12]

'If you believe in media objectivity, then you also believe in Santa Claus,' bemoans senior journalist and editor Smita Prakash at Asian News International (ANI).[13] She was inducted as a member of the PCI by the government in 2018.[14] She says that ANI receives ten to fifteen denials every day from people who are quoted in news stories. In olden times, it was not uncommon, she writes, to feel sorry about a story that had gone wrong; there would be editorial meetings, the journalists would often be taken to task for misreporting or not checking their facts carefully, and the next day, the paper would carry a corrigendum, or an apology. This, she rues, is unthinkable today, as media value systems seem to have changed.[15]

In a new report titled "Untold Stories: How Corruption and Conflicts of Interest Stalk the Newsroom", by the Ethical Journalism Network, an international journalism watchdog, the author for the Indian chapter, A. Panneerselvan, who is also the readers' editor at *The Hindu*, says 'I am acutely aware that of the nearly 100,000 professionals in journalism...a substantial number of individuals and institutions uphold the core values and the cardinal principles of journalism. The exceptions are in a minority, but it's a number sufficient...to colour the popular perception and to undermine public trust.'[16] He refers to the five debilitating problems with the media in India—paid news, opaque private treaties, blatant blackmail, the widening legal regulatory gap and the flawed measurements of audience reach and readership.[17]

What is media objectivity?

Media objectivity is defined by scholars as the detached and unprejudiced gathering and dissemination of news and information. If media writing were objective, it would allow readers and viewers to arrive at decisions about an issue without a journalist's subjective view in influencing the acceptance or rejection of the information provided. Richard F. Taflinger, in his essay "The Myth of Objectivity in Journalism: A Commentary", writes, 'It's a pity that such a goal is impossible to achieve. As long as human beings gather and disseminate news and information, objectivity is an unrealizable dream.'[18]

Why the media in general suffers from a lack of objectivity

Many reasons can be ascribed to the increasing lack of objectivity in media discourse.

- One of the allegations usually levelled at the media is the camouflaging of opinions as news/reporting. It is a rarity these days to see knowledge-based and fact-based reportage. The writer and anchors have no qualms about taking a stand. This is more apparent in news channels than in print.
- Some scholars feel that the media is often guilty of providing misleading definitions of issues, thus giving a slant for readers and viewers to follow.
- Selective choosing of events and issues and avoiding others for various reasons—corporate reasons/client considerations, among others.

- Failing to provide a complete perspective to happenings, thus misleading readers and viewers to contextualize news.
- Distortion of facts, using imperfect research to make a point.
- An inherent bias due to ownership patterns in the media. There are all kinds of inherent interest of the owners—political, corporate, religious and lobbies/associations, to name a few.

Journalistic objectivity is an issue that bothers conscientious journalism practitioners probably as much as it does thinking viewers/readers. Chris Paterson feels that the culture of journalistic objectivity has to be deeply rooted in TV agencies. For instance, in Visnews, the photographers' motto is: 'We do not take sides. We just take pictures.'[19]

Journalist and author Guha Thakurta, mentioned earlier, talks about 'objectivity' and 'being objective' as not being quite the same things. Being objective, he writes, is 'by shedding the shackles of subjective interpretation'. He suggests that if being objective is not always possible, and pure objectivity is theoretically unattainable, journalists could at least simulate objectivity through what he terms as 'ABC'—accuracy, balance and context.[20]

Former *Outlook* editor, the late Vinod Mehta, observed on the disquiet within the media:

> Indian media doesn't do introspection. We recommend it to others—MPs, political parties, militants, judges, scientists…. They are all advised to look deep inside their own trade and clean up the rot. Meanwhile, the rot creeping into the fourth estate is studiously ignored or airbrushed, usually by organizing a "studio discussion" in which the citizen is asked: Does the media need to be accountable? Discussion over. Issue over. Fortunately, even that stratagem is wearing thin. The chicanery is conspicuous.[21]

Media objectivity in times of elections

Elections in democracies are organized with a lot of fanfare and media coverage. There has been a lot of Americanization of elections in many democracies, especially in the developing ones. Scholars have spoken of the tremendous influence of the American style of elections in India and Pakistan over a period of time, especially with the proliferation of news channels. In the sixteenth parliamentary election in India, the campaigning style of Modi was reminiscent of the US presidential style of campaigning.

An election also means a lot of expenditure by political parties and candidates on media publicity, which results in revenue earned by media houses. Who funds the elections is an open secret, but nothing much is written about this aspect in the media. The reason is not far to seek—it is because media happens to be the biggest beneficiary of ad spends during election times.

The last few years in India have witnessed public debate on 'paid media' coverage by some candidates across various political parties during elections. When paid news becomes the practice, media objectivity obviously takes a back seat.

In a meeting of the Editors' Guild in December 2009, the issue of paid news was deliberated upon by members. Sardesai, the president, and Coomi Kapoor, the secretary, sent a signed letter to the member publications 'asking for pledges that his/her publication/TV channel would not carry any paid news, as the practice violates and undermines the principles of free and fair journalism'.[22]

One of the cases that received public attention was when the ECI, in its landmark order, disqualified a sitting MLA, Umlesh Yadav, from Bisauli, UP, for three years under Section 10-A of the Representation of People's Act, 1951, for failing to provide a 'true and correct account' of her election expenses. She was said to have spent money on 'advertisements dressed as news' in two

Hindi newspapers—*Dainik Jagran* and *Amar Ujala*—during the 2007 elections. The case came to the ECI after the PCI adjudicated on a complaint from a losing candidate against the two newspapers for being 'guilty of ethical violations'. In a similar case, the former chief minister of Maharashtra, Ashok Chavan, challenged the ECI's jurisdiction in probing his 2009 poll expenses. The High Court affirmed the ECI's power to do so. In its comment on the ECI's order, *The Hindu* wrote, 'The ECI deserves the highest praise for functioning without fear or favour as the upstanding institution of Indian democracy that it is. The question does pop up, though: What about the newspapers and television channels that enable "defrauding the electorate"?'[23]

In a scathing criticism of the media in Maharashtra around its assembly elections in 2011, development writer P. Sainath in his opinion piece "The Medium, Message and the Money" in *The Hindu* commented that while not all sections of the media could be criticized, quite a few did charge for news from parties and candidates. If there was no money, there was no news. To quote him,

> The Assembly elections saw the culture of 'coverage packages' explode across the State. In many cases, a candidate just had to pay for almost any coverage at all. Issues didn't come into it. No money, no news. This effectively shut out smaller parties and independent voices with low assets and resources. It also misled viewers and readers by denying them any mention of the real issues some of these smaller forces raised.[24]

The piece also talked about candidates complaining of 'extortion' by media houses. Sainath rued the disheartening fact that it was not the small regional newspapers or small channels that did this openly, but the powerful ones. Candidates complained of 'exhortation' but to no avail.[25]

Institutional mechanisms

In various democratic countries, one can find that it's the press and media councils that safeguard the interests of both the media and the people who suffer due to the information published and broadcast in the media. The PCI was first set up in 1966 by the Parliament on the recommendations of the First Press Commission, with the objective of preserving the freedom of the press, and maintaining and improving the standards of the press in India.

The PCI set up a subcommittee[26] comprising Guha Thakurta and K. Sreenivas Reddy to examine the paid news scandal. A report was originally scheduled to be released on 26 April 2010 but was deferred to July 2011 in a 'much watered down' manner, as some council members said that the subcommittee members were worried that the interests and reputation of a few publishers could be hurt in the long run.[27]

The subcommittee, among other things, defined paid news and recommended measures to address the issue. Paid news was defined as 'any news or analysis appearing in any media (print or electronic) for a price in cash or kind as consideration'. Here is a highlight from the PCI report on paid news:

> The election-time paid news phenomenon has three dimensions. One, the reader or the viewer does not get a correct picture of the personality or the performance of the candidate in whose favour or against he decides to cast his vote. This destroys the very essence of democracy. Two, contesting candidates perhaps do not show it in their election expense account, thereby violating the Conduct of Election Rules, 1961, framed by the Election Commission of India under the Representation of the People Act, 1951. Three, those newspapers and television channels which received money in cash but did not disclose it in their official statements of

accounts have violated the Companies Act, 1956, as well as the Income Tax Act, 1961, besides other laws.[28]

Election-time paid news deals are done between candidates, political parties or their agents and the media. The annexure to this chapter carries the recommendations made by the subcommittee to address the 'paid news' menace.

The PCI received adverse comments from senior journalists, including P. Sainath, who wrote in *The Hindu*, as quoted by the *Outlook* magazine:

> To say we have not suppressed the subcommittee's report, we have merely relegated it to our archive for reference, is to add infuriating insult to injury. To praise the authors of the original (as happened in its July 30 meeting) for their effort and then gut the result of that pioneering work, was hypocrisy of a high order. To then present the mangled remains as a guide to fighting paid news eclipses even that benchmark of insincerity. The public surely deserves better. Those publications and channels that were not part of this ugly enterprise of paid news ought to act. For a start, they can put up the 'reference' document on their websites and call public attention to it with headlines, not footnotes.[29]

The issue of paid news in the Indian media has become a topic of discussion in many countries. *The Guardian* reported that the 'paid news phenomenon' violated the ECI rule that limited a candidate's expenditure. Referring to former Maharashtra chief minister Chavan's election to the state assembly, the paper commented that while returns filed by the politician reflected an 'expenditure of just £72 on advertising, stories extolling his achievements appeared for several days in rival newspapers. If the stories had been advertising, as they appeared to be, Chavan's bill would have been many times higher.'[30]

In the meantime, a parliamentary panel asked the I&B Ministry to expeditiously formulate an appropriate policy to curb paid news. In its twelfth report, the standing committee on Information and Technology said that the I&B Ministry had submitted notes to the Law Ministry for amendment in the Representation of People Act and the Press Council Act for examination.[31] As per media reports, a proposal had also been sent to the Law Ministry for examination that the PCI must be fully empowered to adjudicate the complaints of paid news and give a final judgment on the matter.[32] The I&B Ministry is now considering addressing it through 'an amendment in the Press Council Act, which is concerned with standards of newspapers and news agencies in India', as reported by the media. The Bill, however, may lapse with the dissolution of the sixteenth Lok Sabha in 2019.[33]

In its cover story "Paid For News" in 2009, the *Outlook* magazine symbolized the syndrome via a graphic, which said it all. Columnist Anuradha Raman, in the cover story, commented that whether the Indian media admitted it or not, journalism was 'up for sale'. Speaking with many political bigwigs, and quoting former Haryana chief minister Bhupinder Singh Hooda, she wrote that it was common for media houses to ask politicians to 'loosen [their] purse strings if they wanted good press'. It was also common that many politicians paid to get negative stories about rivals published. Former print editor B.G. Verghese, who was a signatory to a complaint to the PCI, spoke about the paid news phenomenon thus, 'It has become an epidemic and has taken the current trend of offering edit space to new levels.'[34] The same sentiment was echoed by others, including UP Chief Minister Yogi Adityanath, then a BJP MP from Gorakhpur. He said, 'Every single newspaper was on sale in my constituency and I was told I had to pay up for publicity.' Husain Dalwai, a Congress spokesperson from Maharashtra, was quoted as saying, 'Nothing was published unless you gave money. In fact, in some media sections, different deals were struck with owners and reporters.'³⁵ Akhilesh Das, a Bahujan Samaj Party (BSP) MP, said without mincing words, 'I don't blame my party if it pays for news in its favour; there is a general bias against my party. Look at how Faizabad bypolls were written about.'³⁶

The story is not different for news channels. They ask for a price for live coverage. They also charge for positive coverage, as shared by Sandeep Dikshit of the Congress, who said that he was approached by a news channel for an hour-long live coverage of Rahul Gandhi's visit to a constituency in Delhi for ₹2.5 lakh.³⁷

While responding to an MP's demand to address paid news, Arun Jaitley, former I&B minister, said during the zero hour in the upper house of the Parliament on 10 May 2016 that though the government supported free speech, the 'aberration' of paid news needed to be checked. Naresh Gujral of the Shiromani Akali Dal (SAD) party commented that the malaise was not restricted to the print media alone but had extended to the electronic media as well. Referring to surveys, he said these were covered by news channels to influence electoral outcome. He described paid news as 'blackmail'.³⁸

The political parties seem to be in campaigning mode even after winning an election. As reported by the media, the BJP is said to have paid for PM Modi's speech at New York's Madison Square Garden in September 2014, which was telecast across Marathi news channels on prime time. To quote Nikhil Wagle of *DNA*, 'BJP leaders conceded they had to pay up to ₹20 lakh per episode, which means the whole deal cost them in crores. The moot question, however, is: Should the media sell its prime-time slot, which is globally reserved only for news, to a political party?'³⁹ Casting aspersions on the media, the columnist further said, 'Corruption is a two-way process. The one who offers money is as guilty as the one who accepts it. Then why does the receiver in this case get away scot-free?'⁴⁰

In an interview with Al Jazeera, Guha Thakurta said, 'The autonomy of the media is meant to facilitate greater accountability of public personalities and reduce corruption. But when the media itself indulges in corrupt practices, especially during election campaigns, it seriously undermines the processes and structures that are meant to uphold and strengthen democracy.'[41]

The PCI issued guidelines in 2010 for the press to regulate itself at the time of elections.

The PCI guidelines 2010

1. It will be the duty of the press to give objective reports about elections and the candidates. The newspapers are not expected to indulge in unhealthy election campaigns, exaggerated reports about any candidate/party or incident during the elections. In practice, two or three closely contesting candidates attract all the media attention. While reporting on the actual campaign, a newspaper may not leave out any important point raised by a candidate and make an attack on his or her opponent.
2. Election campaigns along communal or caste lines are banned under the election rules. Hence, the press should eschew reports that tend to promote feelings of enmity or hatred between people on the ground of religion, race, caste, community or language.
3. The press should refrain from publishing false or critical statements in regard to the personal character and conduct of any candidate or in relation to the candidature or withdrawal of any candidate or his candidature, to prejudice the prospects of that candidate in the elections. The press shall not publish unverified allegations against any candidate/party.
4. The press shall not accept any kind of inducement, financial or otherwise, to project a candidate/party. It shall not accept hospitality or other facilities offered to it by or on behalf of any candidate/party.

5. The press is not expected to indulge in canvassing of a particular candidate/party. If it does, it shall allow the right of reply to the other candidate/party.
6. The press shall not accept/publish any advertisement at the cost of public exchequer regarding achievements of a party/government in power.
7. The press shall observe all the directions/orders/instructions of the Election Commission/Returning Officers or Chief Electoral Officer issued from time to time.

On exit polls
No newspaper shall publish exit-poll surveys, however, genuine they may be, till the last of the polls is over.[42]

When one does a reality check on reporting per se in election times, there is no gainsaying the fact that the PCI guidelines are easily given the go-by by most of the media houses in India.

Media matters

The role of the media is indispensable in democracies, especially during elections. The media helps voters make informed choices while casting their vote. In 2005, the yearly World Press Freedom Day international conference produced a declaration that stressed that 'independent and pluralistic media are essential for ensuring transparency, accountability and participation as fundamental elements of good governance and human rights-based development'. Furthermore, the declaration urged member states to 'respect the function of the news media as an essential factor in good governance, vital to increasing both transparency and accountability in decision-making processes and to communicating the principles of good governance to the citizenry'.[43]

The 2014 parliamentary election received tremendous media coverage. According to the Center for Media Studies (CMS) findings,

> Never before has news media coverage of poll campaign been so polarized (or should we say one-directional), to the extent of predetermining the poll outcome. What started as the AAP's Arvind Kejriwal-centric media coverage (at the announcement of the poll schedule) became Modi-driven too soon and remained that way till the poll campaign ended. Although the fight at the national level was between the incumbent Congress-party-led UPA and the BJP, the media coverage of the Congress party was not even 30 per cent at any point of the campaign. Even the coverage of Rahul Gandhi by news channels was only about 10 per cent of the prime time given to Modi. It was interesting how Kejriwal's campaign was relegated to third position as the poll schedule advanced, phase after phase.[44]

On news channels conducting opinion polls, the CMS research observed that never before were there so many prepolls and exit polls conducted by news channels as in 2014. Some channels presented more than two prepoll surveys within just two weeks. Most of the surveys had similar projections of the poll outcome. National channels, as well as regional channels, irrespective of their language, conducted poll surveys in 2014. All these surveys were promoted by channels and ran anywhere between thirty minutes to two hours. To quote from the CMS research,

> The punditry nature of channels [and their experts] was unleashed by way of studio discussions, and some even taking to the field to put forward the survey findings to a larger public [for endorsements!]. The question here is, with so much resources [by channels themselves or someone else bearing the expenditure], and so much broadcast time for their

coverage, what impact or implications could be attributed? Can poll surveys of channels be credited for voter turnout, or for a single party emerging victorious, or for creating a 'Modi wave'? Then, of course, are the questions of transparency of surveys, their methodologies and about the identity of the agency, which conducted the field work. Paid news in the context of elections has been talked about for quite some time. But no one has talked about 'paid surveys' of channels![45]

In summation, it can be said that with so many cross-currents and undercurrents, no discussion on media objectivity can be conclusive. It depends on where the argument is coming from. The issue is debated, discussed and critiqued in the public domain, more so with the coming of social media platforms and huge user-generated communication on the Internet. It sure is not going away anytime soon, but it is hoped that the people as media consumers will decide what to watch and read.

Annexure

Suggestions from the PCI subcommittee comprising Paranjoy Guha Thakurta and K. Sreenivas Reddy.

- The Press Council of India should constitute a body of media professionals with wide representation at the national/state/district levels to investigate (either suo moto or on receipt of complaints) instances of 'paid news' and the recommendations of such a body—after going through an appellate mechanism—should be binding on the Election Commission of India and other government authorities.
- Self-regulation is the best option to check the 'paid news' phenomenon. However, self-regulation only offers partial solutions to the problem, since there will always be offenders

who will refuse to abide by voluntary codes of conduct and ethical norms that are not legally mandated. There should be a debate among all concerned stakeholders on whether a directive of the Supreme Court of India that enjoins television channels to stop broadcasting campaign-related information on candidates and political parties forty-eight hours before elections take place can and should be extended to the print medium, since such a restriction does not apply to this section of the media at present.

- Efforts should be made to educate the voters to differentiate between doctored reporting, and balanced and just reporting. This can be done by the Ministry of Information & Broadcasting with the help of the Press Council of India and various associations of journalists and newspaper owners.
- The Union Information & Broadcasting Ministry should conduct national conferences, workshops, seminars and awareness-generating campaigns involving, among others, the Press Council of India, the Election Commission of India, representatives of editors, journalist associations and unions, political parties and media owners to deliberate on the issue and arrive at workable solutions to curb the paid news' phenomenon in particular.
- The Union I&B Minister should hold separate meetings with national associations of newspaper owners, editors and journalists to discuss the 'paid news' phenomenon and how it should be curbed. A meeting of all political parties should also be organised to make them understand that if the phenomenon of 'paid news' is not checked, no political party will benefit. Similarly, owners of media companies should be made to understand that money illegally obtained for 'paid news' is not just myopic but

will eventually lead to loss of credibility among readers and viewers, and will, hence, be detrimental to the interests of the media.

▸ A small committee of Members of Parliament from both houses should hold a hearing for suggesting changes in the Representation of the People Act 1951 to prevent the practice of paying for news coverage in newspapers and television channels and declaring it as an 'electoral malpractice' or an act of corruption and be made a punishable offence. All these initiatives, if sincerely implemented, may not entirely stop such malpractices in the Indian media but could reduce their incidence to a considerable extent.

Recommendations:
1) Representation of the People Act, 1951, be amended to make incidence of paid news a punishable electoral malpractice.
2) The Press Council of India be fully empowered to adjudicate the complaints of 'paid news' and give final judgment in the matter.
3) The Press Council Act be amended to make its recommendations binding and electronic media be brought under its purview, and
4) The Press Council of India be reconstituted to include representatives from electronic and other media.

Notes

1. Brants, Kees, and Volymer, Katrin, quoting from earlier works (Brants, 1998; Franklin, 1997; Sparks & Tulloch, 2000) in their edited book *Political Communication in Postmodern Democracy: Challenging the Primacy of Politics*, Palgrave Macmillan, 2011, New York

2. Ibid
3. Herman, Edward S., and Chomsky, Noam, *Manufacturing Consent: The Political Economy of the Mass Media*, Pantheon Books, New York, 1988, pp.18–19
4. Ibid
5. Sigal, Leon, *Reporters and Officials: The Organization of Politics and Newsmaking*, Heath, Washington DC, 1973, p.69
6. https://en.oxforddictionaries.com/word-of-the-year/word-of-the-year-2016
7. "The Post-Truth World: Yes, I'd Lie To You", *The Economist*, 10 September 2016
   https://www.economist.com/briefing/2016/09/10/yes-id-lie-to-you
8. Patterson, Thomas E., *Informing the News: The Need for Knowledge-Based Journalism*, Vintage Books, New York, 2013
9. Sardesai, Rajdeep, "Modi and Me", *Mint*, 3 November 2014, p.7
10. http://archive.financialexpress.com/news/promodi-supporters-beat-up-tv-anchor-rajdeep-sardesai-outside-madison-square-garden/1293852?rhheader
11. Hohmann, James, "The Daily 202: Why Trump Won—and Why the Media Missed It", *The Washington Post*, 9 November 2016
    https://www.washingtonpost.com/news/powerpost/paloma/daily-202/2016/11/09/daily-202-why-trump-won-and-whythe-media-missed-it/5822ea17e9b69b6085905dee/?utm_term=.792ca57a281d
12. Desai, Santosh, "The Mystery of the Invisible Wave?", in his column "City City Bang Bang", *The Times of India*, 13 March 2017
13. Prakash, Smita, "The Myth of Objectivity in Media", *Mid-day*, 2 December 2013
    http://www.mid-day.com/articles/the-myth-of-objectivity-inmedia/242766
14. Dutta, Amrita N., "Not a Single Journalist Has Got a Fresh Govt Accreditation Since March", The Print, 17 December 2018
    https://theprint.in/governance/not-a-single-journalist-has-got-a-fresh-govt-accreditation-since-march/164885/

15. Prakash, Smita, "The Myth of Objectivity in Media", *Mid-day*, 2 December 2013
    http://www.mid-day.com/articles/the-myth-of-objectivity-inmedia/242766
16. Narayanan, Nayantara, "Five Ethical Problems That Plague Indian Journalism", Scroll.in, 19 March 2015
    https://scroll.in/article/714570/five-ethical-problems-that-plagueindian-journalism
17. Ibid
18. http://public.wsu.edu/~taflinge/mythobj.html
19. http://theviewspaper.net/is-objectivity-a-myth/
20. Thakurta, Paranjoy G., *Media Ethics*, Second Edition, Oxford University Press, New Delhi, 2012, pp.75–76
21. Mehta, Vinod, "Please Do Not Sell", *Outlook*, 21 December 2009
    http://www.outlookindia.com/article/please-do-not-sell/263241
22. http://www.easternpanorama.in/index.php/web-special/881-paid-news-the-bane-of-ethical-journalism
23. "Paid News Claims Its Price", *The Hindu*, 21 October 2011
    http://www.thehindu.com/opinion/editorial/paid-news-claims-itsprice/article2559714.ece
24. Sainath, P., "The Medium, Message and the Money", *The Hindu*, 26 October 2009
    http://www.thehindu.com/opinion/columns/sainath/the-mediummessage-and-the-money/article38482.ece
25. Ibid
26. The PCI appointed a subcommittee comprising Paranjoy Guha Thakurta and Kalimekolan Sreenivas Reddy on 9 June 2009 'to examine the phenomenon of paid news observed during the last Lok Sabha elections...based on inputs received from the members and others'. The two members met a cross-section of society in New Delhi, Mumbai and Hyderabad, and also went through many letters and representations that were sent to the council. The PCI, in its two meetings held in Indore and New Delhi on 31 March 2010 and

26 April 2010, respectively, discussed the report of the subcommittee in detail. Members gave a number of suggestions and, thereafter, the PCI chairman appointed a drafting committee to prepare a final report for the consideration of the council. The chairman appointed a twelve-member committee consisting of H.N. Cama, Lalit Mangotra, U.C. Sharma, Y.C. Halan, K. Sreenivas Reddy, Kalyan Barooah, S.N. Sinha, Anil Jugal Kishore Agarwal, Kundn R.L. Vyas, Paranjoy Guha Thakurta, P. Javadekar and Keshav Rao.

27. Thakurta, Paranjoy G., and Reddy, K. Sreenivas, "Paid News: The Buried Report", *Outlook*, 6 August 2010
28. http://presscouncil.nic.in/OldWebsite/CouncilReport.pdf
29. Thakurta, Paranjoy G., and Reddy, K. Sreenivas, "Paid News: The Buried Report", *Outlook*, 6 August 2010
30. Rahman, Maseeh, "India: 'Paid News' Scandal Hits Major Newspapers", *The Guardian*, 4 January 2010 https://www.theguardian.com/media/2010/jan/04/india-paid-news-scandal
31. "Parliament Panel Asks I&B Ministry to Form Policy to Curb Paid News", *The Economic Times*, 13 August 2015 https://economictimes.indiatimes.com/news/politics-and-nation/parliament-panel-asks-ib-ministry-to-form-policy-to-curb-paidnews/articleshow/48473084.cms
32. "Govt Mulls Moves to Make Paid News Punishable Malpractice", *DNA*, 12 August 2015 http://www.dnaindia.com/india/report-govt-mulls-moves-to-makepaid-news-punishable-malpractice-2113846
33. Ranjan, Amitav, "I&B to Drop Paid News Regulation in Draft Bill", *The Indian Express*, 14 December 2018 https://indianexpress.com/article/india/information-and-broadcasting-to-drop-paid-news-regulation-in-draft-bill-newspapers-magazines-5492867/
34. Raman, Anuradha, "News You Can Abuse", *Outlook*, 21 December 2009

35. Ibid
36. Ibid
37. Ibid
38. "MPs Unite Against Paid News Scourge", *Hindustan Times*, 11 May 2016 http://www.hindustantimes.com/india/mps-unite-against-paid-newsscourge/story-yt7VpGgSs2Vs115Mcp7tyO.html
39. Wagle, Nikhil, "The Growing Cancer of Paid News", *DNA*, 17 October 2014
40. Ibid
41. Umar, Baba, "Paid News Clouds India Elections", Aljazeera.com, 21 April 2014 https://www.aljazeera.com/indepth/features/2014/04/paid-news-clouds-india-elections-2014416121619668302.html
42. http://presscouncil.nic.in/OldWebsite/NORMS-2010.pdf
43. http://www.unesco.org/new/en/unesco/events/prizes-and-celebrations/celebrations/international-days/world-press-freedom-day/previous-celebrations/worldpressfreedomday200900000/dakar-declaration/
44. http://www.cmsindia.org/publications/Monograph_Coverage_2014_LokSabha_Polls.pdf
45. Ibid

4

THE INCONGRUENT MILLIONS AS VOTERS AND MEDIA AUDIENCES: IMPACT ON ELECTIONS

> 'One of the penalties for refusing to participate in politics is that you end up being governed by your inferiors.'
> —PLATO

When Abraham Lincoln said, 'Democracy is the government of the people, by the people, for the people', it perhaps was wishful thinking on his part. Over the years, it has been realized that, often, those elected to serve the people as public servants become so inebriated with power that the people who elected them become the last thing on their priority list—till they need them again to win the next election. The people as voters are so cajoled, persuaded and misled on various ploys and heightened media stimuli that one wonders if the people as voters use their franchise on informed choices. One thing, however, is certain: An election gives a sense of 'being' to the average voter.

Empirical studies provide interesting data on Indians as voters. In a country with more than 900 million voters to elect more than 500 Lok Sabha members and a few thousand state assembly members; with a few millions living below the poverty line, struggling to eke out a living for themselves; and where a large number of people are non-literate and often at the receiving end of the corruption, nepotism and inefficiency of their elected representatives and an equally wishy-washy bureaucracy, there is still something to be celebrated. India, all said and done, is a robust democracy, much to the chagrin of Western analysts. Election times are seen as times of hope and aspiration for candidates and voters alike.

In a path-breaking judgement, the apex court, in January 2017, ruled that seeking votes in the name of caste, race, community or language by a candidate, his agent or anyone in his name would be treated as corrupt electoral practice, rendering the person open to disqualification. The order also said that a candidate would be disqualified if an appeal were made by a religious leader to vote for him/her. As soon as the order came, sceptics in the government and political circles, however, felt that it had limited utility, given the complexities and long litigation process.[1]

People as voters

Article 326 of the Indian Constitution grants universal adult suffrage, according to which every adult citizen is entitled to cast his/her vote in all state elections, unless he/she is 'convicted of certain criminal offences' or 'deemed unsound of mind'. As per this concept, the right to vote is not restricted by caste, race, sex, religion or financial status.[2]

In retrospect, in pre-Independence times, only 13 per cent Indians had the right to vote. The Motilal Nehru Committee had recommended universal suffrage for all Indians. Later, in 1928, when Dr B.R. Ambedkar appeared before the Simon Commission and insisted on incorporating universal adult franchise in the Constitution of India, while reiterating that elections were 'a weapon in the hands of the most oppressed sections of society' and voting rights would give them politico-legal equality, it was an assertion on behalf of the teeming millions.[3]

Being a multicultural, multilinguistic and multireligious society, beset with social inequity, economic divide and unequal media access and exposure, elections in India invariably reflect the gullibility of the voters. Parties often divide the electorate based on religion, caste, creed, and rural and urban demographics. Political parties exploit these vulnerabilities openly in their campaigns. The campaigns are positioned on these premises, either supporting or deriding one or more factors. For instance, *'Jaat pe na paat pe, mohar lagegi haath pe'* (Neither on caste nor on creed, people are going to stamp their votes on the 'hand'), was the slogan of the Congress under the leadership of P.V. Narasimha Rao in the 1996 election. In the 1989 election, the BJP campaign exhorted voters to not be ashamed but be proud of their Hindu identity.

As India has a large segment of young voters, the last few elections have seen political parties trying to influence them on aspirational grounds. It was not uncommon to find parties enticing young voters, especially first-timers, with aspirational products. For example, in UP, laptops were promised and, on victory, laptops were distributed free of cost to hundreds of thousands of youth. In Bihar, cycles were given to young girls so they could pedal to school. Such strategies paid rich political dividends to the parties.

In the popular programme *Aap Ki Adalat* on India TV, anchor Rajat Sharma quizzed former UP chief minister Akhilesh Yadav ahead of the UP elections in February 2017 on his promise to distribute smartphones to the youth if he came to power. To this, Yadav nonchalantly replied that there was nothing wrong with that promise, as the last election time was of laptops and the next would be of smartphones, rounding off his reply with a sarcastic question to the anchor himself: Was his action not in tune with the PM's call for Digital India?

Deconstructing the Indian electorate

According to Census 2011, of India's 1.21 billion population, 833 million lived in rural India and 377 million in urban India; 31.2 per cent of the total population lived in urban centres, compared with the 27.8 per cent in 2001 and the 25.5 per cent in 1991.[4]

The latest data on population and age structure as of 2016 provide interesting findings, as reflected in the table below:[5]

Population	1,266,883,598 (July 2016 est.)
Age structure	0–14 years: 27.71% (male 186,420,229/female 164,611,755) 15–24 years: 17.99% (male 121,009,850/female 106,916,692) 25–54 years: 40.91% (male 267,203,029/female 251,070,105) 55–64 years: 7.3% (male 46,398,574/female 46,105,489) 65 years and above: 6.09% (male 36,549,003/female 40,598,872)5

Source: India Demographics Profile 2018, Index Mundi

People in the age group of 25–54 years comprise about 41 per cent of the electorate. This electorate, along with about 10 per cent of first-time voters—or 12 crore youth—remain the most important constituency for any political party to reach out to. Over 41 per cent of the population in India speaks Hindi, so poll managers have to factor in this reality in the choice of media and linguistic strategies. English may be spoken by only about 10 per cent of the population, but these are the people who matter the most in the decision-making process—they belong to the policy echelons, they are often the rich and the elite, and they are metro inhabitants. Therefore, parties make full use of the English media to reach out to this niche but valuable constituency.

The last couple of decades have seen an improvement in the life of the average Indian. According to the Housing Census data for 2011, people in rural India saw significant improvement in the quality of houses they lived in, and access to water and banking facilities, with a little over one in two households having access to a bank, as compared to a little less than one in three in the 2001 census. To quote government sources, by 2017, banks had opened 17.74 crore accounts under the Pradhan Mantri Jan Dhan Yojana with a total deposit of more than ₹22,000 crore.

Why do people vote?

People have different interest levels in general and for using their franchise in particular. William H. Flanigan and Nancy N. Zingale ascribe five factors to the differences in the level of voter interest. The authors' referral point is the US presidential election, but it can hold good for other democracies as well:[6]

- Difference in media coverage in a given election
- Significance attached by voters to the office
- Importance of issues raised in the campaign
- Attractiveness of the candidate
- Competitiveness of the contest

According to Angus Campbell, variations in these factors are called 'high stimulus' and 'low stimulus'.[7]

For long, media scholars, who have studied media behaviour of the public, have found a close relationship between their interest level in politics and the attention to political stimulus through the mass media. The phenomenon has several consequences in political communication. The most interested in politics may also be partisan and loyalists to a certain political ideology. This can lead such persons to seek more political information about the concerned candidate or the political party of their choice. Such a category of electorate is more likely to retain and use new elements of information than the apathetic and the inattentive. Some of the studies suggest that through a process of filtration and selective perception, they only retain the information that reinforces their existing belief patterns. The impact of the media, the research suggests, is likely to be greatest when the recipients of messages have little information and few existing attitudes.[8]

People as consumers of goods, products, services and media programmes are important in the sociopolitical framework. Their constant interaction with each other at various levels results in the formation of public opinion on issues that concern them as individuals, as members of a race, class, caste and religious belief, and as consumers of various brands, besides being citizens and voters. Therefore, for governments, political parties, marketers and the media, the public and its opinion decide how these institutions will fare. It is not uncommon to find opinion polling on various issues conducted by media houses, political parties and consumer research marketers to know the pulse of the public.

Defining people as media audience and as voters

Are people a faceless mass, mere statistical data? Is the power of public opinion a myth or a reality? Questions such as these have been raised from time to time, but history is witness to the power of the people and the triumph of public opinion time and again. The freedom struggles in many countries, including India, the battle for civil liberties in the West, the call against apartheid in South Africa, the Tiananmen Square Massacre in China and the Arab Spring in the Middle East are just a few of many examples to vindicate this argument. No despot, no dictator could contain the power of the people and the surge of public opinion for long. People are the axis around which democratic institutions function and progress. People as consumers in marketing terms, people as the target audience in media terms and people as voters in a democracy are the bedrock upon which these institutions are founded and sustained. If the elections in India are any indication, the power of the people is most manifest when they decide to cast their vote. The mightiest have bitten the dust at the hands of voters. They have also bounced back because the same voters either thought they deserved a second chance or because the ones they had elected did not live up to their expectations. There is nothing permanent in politics.

For long, the thinking among political analysts has been that when people choose to vote, the motivation is usually the same. But now some researchers of the Indian elections have come up with newer insights. What motivates a voter to cast his/her vote? For some, it may be a matter of 'right' that needs to be exercised; for others, a vote can be seen as their belief in a candidate, in the hope that he/she will fulfil his/her promises and voters' expectations. The third dimension of the vote can be seen in its 'power to transform and power to change'. From an extraneous perspective, a larger voter turnout reflects people's faith in democracy with all its imperfections.[9]

India has the largest electorate in the world, with over 800 million voters. Political parties use various kinds of media vigorously to reach out to the voter base. Interestingly, there are more than 1,900 parties in India, by far the largest number when compared with democracies across the world. It is a different matter that 400 registered parties have not fought any election, as per a media report based on an input from the ECI.[10]

The media is relevant in the electoral process for a variety of reasons, such as for its function as a watchdog, as a campaign platform, as a forum in the public domain for discussions and deliberations and as a public educator of issues and concerns.

The 'mass' in mass communication

Is 'mass' in the mass media the same as the potential voters in an election? How are the audiences segmented for an election? Is it the same way programmers segment media audiences? This area of study in mass communication needs to cover the dynamics and interrelations among messages, mediums and audiences.

People of various demographic profiles, known as audiences, are referred to as the 'mass' in the context of the mass media. The term 'mass' has different connotations in sociological, economic, political and media contexts.

The element of large-scale (mass) dissemination of ideas was present even when there were no mass media. The masses were reached through meetings, congregations, word of mouth, inscriptions and the grapevine. Relics from the time of the Indian king Ashoka—the iron pillars with the teachings of Lord Buddha inscribed on them—have stood the test of time and can be seen even after more than 2,000 years. King Ashoka also spread Buddhism in many countries through his emissaries. This was largely independent of any media, in the contemporary sense of the term.

With the advent of newspapers and radio in the past century, the power of mass-circulated dailies and the impact of audio was realized and acted upon. Hitler and his crony Joseph Goebbels looked at information as an instrument of social control. The Nazi state machinery unleashed unbridled propaganda through underground radio stations in Allied countries that were at war with Germany. Later, cinema and television created a larger-than-life image for viewers. The power of the audio-visual medium on the psyche of viewers has been a subject of much empirical research. The coming of the Internet and various social media platforms have further redefined the meaning of the masses in the context of the media. If the past few elections in the West and in India are any indication, there is no denying the fact that the Internet and its reach have changed the way elections are strategized, especially in liberal democracies. Candidates through social media platforms, especially Facebook and Twitter, now easily reach out to people, especially the young electorate. PM Modi, when contesting the 2014 election, made vigorous use of social media. Modi, as per media reports, is the world's most followed or liked world leader on two social media platforms—Facebook and Instagram. He is No.3 on Twitter. Modi tops the list of 50 most followed world leaders on Facebook, as his official page is liked by over 43.2 million people.[11] Modi has used Twitter for campaigns such as #MakeInIndia, #SwachBharat, #MannKiBaat and #SelfieWithDaughter to connect with citizens.

Anatomy of media audiences

An individual or collective group of people who read or consume any media text can be defined as an audience. For example, radio listeners, television viewers, newspaper and magazine readers, and traffic on websites also qualify as media audiences or netizens.

Types of audience

Audience in the media context can be defined as follows:

Mass audience: Often termed 'broadcast audience', mass audiences are those who consume mainstream or popular texts such as soaps or sitcoms that target a large group of people (women, men, children, senior citizens, etc.).

Niche audience: This is much smaller but very influential. A niche audience is a small, select group of people with a singular interest. As we have seen, there are mass entertainment channels, such as Sony, Star and Colors, which telecast various genres of entertainment programmes to cater to a wide variety of audiences. On the other hand, there are niche channels such as Fashion TV, Good Life, Epic, National Geographic and History that attract niche audiences. Similarly, some examples of niche publications could be magazines and periodicals catering exclusively to a certain audience group. For instance, *Bird Watcher's Digest*, *Economic & Political Weekly* and *Seminar* would qualify as niche magazines.

Why is the audience important?

There is a symbiotic relationship between the media and its audience. If there were no audience, there would be no media, in the real sense of the term. Media organizations produce media texts and programmes to reach out to a wide cross-section of the audience. The more the reach of the TV programme, the more the target rating point (TRP) and the more the ad revenue for the media house. Similarly, more readers would mean more circulation and readership figures, and so higher ad revenue for the print media house. In this context, the audience becomes a very important player in the media arithmetic.

Audience fragmentation

Traditional media like newspapers, television and the radio have benefitted from a large audience base, but with the branching out of the media and a variety of mediums to choose from, there has been a fragmentation of the audience. It is also a fact that digital technology has led to increasing uncertainty over how we define an audience. In traditional media like television, the premise is that a large audience is expected to watch a programme at the same time, but with digital media, especially with the Internet, where one accesses information as and when needed or convenient, the definition of mass audience (reached out to at the same time) has undergone a tremendous change.

A more tech-savvy audience

Most changes in the media in the recent past have been technology-driven, enabling the audience to be active and interactive with it. The web has also facilitated the ease of accessing news and other programmes at the convenience of the media user. The younger audiences don't seem to use classic media the way the older generation does. Instead of the linear format of classic media, the digital media, especially audio-visual content on the Internet, is in a nonlinear format, which enables the audience to navigate and access information in whichever manner it wishes to, without going through the entire gamut of materials available in a linear fashion. At the annual Confederation of Indian Industry (CII) conference on Media and Entertainment in October 2015, a focus group research was shared, which, among other things, reflected that the Indian youth accessed information, news and various genres of entertainment programmes, including films and serials, increasingly on the Internet, and often via their smartphones and iPads. The reasons cited were the ease of accessing and convenience using a nonlinear format. With a range of uncensored overseas programmes available on the Internet, the youth preferred it over television, the study revealed.[12]

With more than 100 crore mobile phones in the country, media planners could not have asked for more during election time. The AAP was probably the first to reach out digitally to people, not only for its messages but also for inviting them to road shows and crowdsourcing during the Delhi elections in 2013 and 2015. The BJP in 2009 made an innovative use of mobile-phone advertising by using Atal Bihari Vajpayee's voice for soliciting votes for the party.

The audience in marketing terms

Referred to as the target audience, market researchers broadly segment the audience on two parameters—demographics and psychographics. Let's understand both the terms closely.

Demographics: The segmenting of the prospective audience through demographic profiling based on age, sex, income, occupation, education, household income, etc.

Psychographics: The segmenting of the target audience on the basis of lifestyle, attitudes, beliefs, value systems, personality type, buying motives and/or extent of product usage. Most media products are created with a 'typical' audience member, often with a psychographic profile in view.

One of the challenges that psychographic research faces is that researchers have to rely on consumers' own descriptions of their psychological characteristics or attitudes. Perceptions or the understanding of various characteristics differ from person to person. If respondents are asked to rate themselves on their ambitiousness on a scale of one to five—one being 'not at all' and five being 'very ambitious'—the term 'ambition' is perceived differently by different people. But when a question related to demographics, such as the respondents' age, say between 18–24 and 25–34, is asked, the parameters mean the same to everyone. There is no problem in respondents' understanding of the question—but in the former case, individual perceptions will come into play when responding.[13]

Is there an average Indian voter?

How does one describe the quintessential Indian voter? How do various demographic and psychographic groupings segregate among the political parties?

There may not be a straightjacketed definition for the average voter, but there is no denying the fact that the Indian voter has evolved and understands the value of his/her vote.

Milan Vaishnav's seminal research on Indian political economy, which included the study of the 2014 election, brings to notice some interesting findings. He argues that despite the 2014 election being a watershed moment in the voting behaviour of Indians, upon closer examination, one found the reinforcement of old behaviour in many areas, some of which included dynastic politicians continuing to win elections, with one in five who made it to the Parliament from the same political family; and alleged criminals continuing to fight and win seats, which meant that the voters went for those they believed could get things done, irrespective of who they really were. Although there was a general perception of regional parties becoming important in national politics, the results reinforced that this was not really the case. There was a fair balance between national and regional parties in the electoral outcome. Another interesting insight was that though social biases remained entrenched in India, the transmission of those biases into the political domain was imperfect and could, to some extent, have been weakening.[14]

In 'public interest'

The ECI and the governments at the central and state levels in the past have run campaigns exhorting people to vote and make informed choices. The corporate sector in the past has also pitched in. A high-visibility campaign, Jaago Re (Wake Up), was mounted by the Tata Group through its flagship brand Tata Tea (now Tata Global Beverages) in 2007 for its various tea products, probably little realizing that its strong message to the youth to wake up from its slumber and vote in the 2009 election would catch the imagination of the entire nation. The company also had a website in place for voter registration (www.jaagore.com), which helped people with an easy, step-by-step process. The website, according to company sources, got 28 lakh registrations and 6 lakh first-time voters. Out of the 28 lakh registrations, one-fourth converted to actual voters.[15] Idea Cellular also picked up election-based issues in its Kya Idea Hai, Sirji! (What an Idea, Sirji!) campaign.

The media's influence on the audience as voters

The media plays the role of a catalyst and acts as a link between political parties and voters. The audience, in the absence of mediating institutions, is believed to be easily open to the influence of the media by being passive recipients of media messages. 'Mass society theory,' according to authors Stanley J. Baran and Dennis K. Davis, 'is an idea that media has strong influence towards people, it plays a role of shaping people's mind and perception of the social world and it is also to manipulate people's action with delicate, subtle and effective ways.'[16] Mass society theory, at the same time, gives primacy to the media as a maintainer of mass society. This theory emphasizes the dominant media model and gives primacy to the media as a causal factor, invoking images of manipulation and control.

The criticism against the media, especially the news media, as earlier mentioned, has been that it does not verily tell the audience *what to think* but *what to think about*. News media, thus, sets the agenda and prioritizes parts of the world, telling the audience what is more important and what is not. Many images that the audiences carry in their heads do not necessarily belong to the real world. The media images can be about a variety of issues, places, countries and people the audience may never have seen, situations it may never have faced and issues it may never have thought about. Therefore, invariably, the media becomes socially, culturally, politically and economically important in influencing the lives of its readers and viewers in more complex ways than one may think.

Many scholars consider social desirability to be another key component in the formation of public opinion. This argument postulates that people in general form their opinions based on what they believe is the popular opinion. Stimulated by media messages over various channels, especially social media, perceptions get reinforced as gospels of truth, which more and more people tend to believe in. The fact that the media is a major source of information has left social scientists scared that it can have an adverse impact on vulnerable minds, especially youngsters.

Public opinion polls in election time

The last few decades have seen an increasing investment in opinion polls by political parties and media houses. Opinion polls can be entertaining to those engaged in it, but have been a cause for great concern to political scientists, sociologists and civil society at large.

Do opinion polls have a decisive role to play in elections? Is their power in politics a reality, an exaggeration or a myth? While there can be no definitive answers to this, there is no denying the fact that electoral politics over the years has become a booming business, and opinion polls—by all kinds of interests, including market researchers, political parties and the media—have become a harsh reality. Critics of opinion polls believe that whenever opinion polls are publicized, there could be a 'bandwagon' or 'underdog' impact—which results in people choosing to side with the probable winner, so as not to waste their vote, and the one appearing to be losing not being able to garner as much voter support as they otherwise may have.

Concerned about this impact, many countries have drawn up guidelines on when opinion poll agencies can share information with the electorate. The ECI has also debarred the publicizing of exit poll results until all the constituencies have completed polling.

Polls can go wrong, and have gone wrong more times than one can count. Dr Gallup, who pioneered opinion polling and made a fortune from it, had incorrectly predicted former US president Franklin Roosevelt's win by 7 per cent. Roosevelt won with 55 per cent of the vote, compared to the 62 per cent predicted by Dr Gallup. Again, in 1948, though Dr Gallup's error was only

4.5 per cent, it predicted the wrong winner. Dewy lost by 4 per cent, while the polling agency had forecast his victory by 5 per cent. Pollsters have gone wrong many times, the latest example being in the US election of 2016—but why does it happen?

Experts believe that the errors are more profound now for various reasons, which include vested interests sponsoring opinion polls, allegations of data fudging, market researchers engaged for opinion polls who may be good at quantitative research techniques but are not necessarily experts in gauging the dynamics and undercurrents of elections, and voter behaviour, which is dependent on many factors, including survey technique, the research universe, sample size, spread and the quality of field researchers. Voting for a party or a candidate is not like buying a brand or switching to another brand. Many factors account for the choice of the average voter in India. One has to factor in family, caste, gender, religion and economic status, besides the publicity gimmicks unleashed by various political parties and the role played by the news media and opinion poll agencies. Early opinion polling in India has seen the 'horse race' aspect of election, thus discouraging serious and honest politicians from contesting and also possibly dissuading some voters from using their franchise.

The US presidential election in 2016 proved to be a grand failure for the media and opinion polling, as they all went grotesquely wrong in their assessment of the ground reality!

In the assembly polls in India conducted in February-March 2017, most opinion polls and exit polls misjudged the extent of the mandate the BJP had received in UP. In fact, the media and the pollsters did not talk of any 'wave' at all. What one read in newspapers and saw on prime-time bulletins was talk of a 'close fight' between the BJP and the SP-Congress combine. Some even said that the dark horse, the BSP, could spring a surprise. Social commentator Santosh Desai said after the assembly results, 'How did such a big wave pass unnoticed? There are some who argue that this is the result of a deliberate slant of the media, which makes it prone to downplaying the appeal that Modi generates among people. And a significant section of media works hard at undermining the efforts of the government, and hence is unable to see any good in its action, the theory goes...however, a lot of sympathetic media also did not see the wave.'[17]

There is a feeling among pollsters that India in general is a difficult country for conducting opinion polls due to its diversity and other ground realities. Selecting a sample for polls raises special problems, given that 70 per cent of the electorate resides in the rural hinterland, some of the areas being inaccessible and media-dark. A sample size of 1,000 may suffice in the West, but due to social, cultural and economic heterogeneity, the sample size in India has to be much larger. If we were to compare the opinion polling techniques between India and the West, most research is conducted in the West telephonically, but until the last few years—when there was a huge spurt in mobile connectivity—research was through face-to-face interaction. In India, it has been seen that research agencies often depend on the village headmen for approaching villagers—it is a common sight to find respondents echoing the opinions of the headmen. It is quite possible that they may vote later according to their own choice, thus creating a reality gap.

Marketing and Research Group (MARG), a research agency in India that has conducted many opinion polls, attempted to create a simulated situation by carrying a fictitious 'ballot box', with respondents being given a slip of paper that resembled a ballot paper to stamp on their preferred candidate/party. This served two purposes—it reduced the respondents' fear of exposing his/her choice and allowed them privacy.

A common problem faced by pollsters is the great difference in the issues between rural and urban voters in India. The failure of both the India Shining and the Bharat Nirman campaigns can be cited as examples, when these resonated differently with the urban and rural electorate.

Electronic Voting Machines (EVMs) were introduced in some parts of India from the 1999 general election, and in totality since 2014 for both the general and the state elections. From time to time, some, especially the losing candidates and parties, have raised the issue of the machines being tampered with, former BSP president Mayawati being one after the results of the April 2017 UP elections were announced. AAP head Kejriwal was also vocal about the alleged tampering of the EVMs during the Punjab election in 2017, as reported widely by the media.[18] His line of argument was that in some constituencies, the AAP did not even get votes equivalent to the number of party volunteers and workers there. The party, as per media reports, has also submitted a letter to the ECI complaining about it. The party, it is believed, has demanded that slips generated by the Voter Verifiable Paper Audit Trail (VVPAT) machines be matched with the papers generated by the EVMs to verify the Punjab assembly election results.[19]

After a ruling by the Delhi High Court and the Supreme Court, and demands from various political parties, the ECI as a pilot project introduced the VVPAT system in eight parliamentary constituencies in the 2014 general election, making the process transparent and secure.[20]

As the cost of political campaigns has been on the rise, investment in an honest and professionally valid opinion research needs to be addressed seriously by parties and candidates, both for mapping public perceptions about them and getting their campaigns right, and for keeping an eye on competitors' plans and strategies and gauging their impact on the electorate.

In the following paragraphs, we shall take a case study of how the BJP targeted the voters, resulting in a resounding victory for the party.

Case study: How the BJP targeted the electorate for the sixteenth parliamentary election in 2014

An analysis of the BJP's performance in the 2014 general election, drawing on the Centre for the Study of Developing Societies (CSDS) post-poll survey data, suggests that the party cobbled together disparate support sources from across the social spectrum—though a glaring exception was the minority Muslim community.

The CSDS post-election poll in caste-conscious UP, for instance, showed that the BJP had won as many as 45 per cent of the non-Jatav Dalit vote, despite the Jatavs being the core Dalit supporters of the rival BSP. Similarly, in neighbouring Bihar, the BJP performed well among those sections of the Other Backward Classes (OBC) that had previously voted for the BJP's erstwhile ally in the state—the Janata Dal (United), or the JD(U). However, the state elections of 2015 had a different impact altogether, as the electoral strategies of the JD(U) and the Rashtriya Janata Dal (RJD) proved to be too much for the BJP.

One obvious driver of these results was the polarization of the Hindu-Muslim votes, thanks to the Hindu majoritarian rhetoric of the BJP and the Sangh Parivar, and their alleged tactics at mobilizing the voters along communal lines. Clearly, this sort of polarization was an important aspect of the BJP's election campaign, even if it was not necessarily its cornerstone on a pan-Indian basis. It is hard to quantify the precise impact of this approach, as many voters may not willingly disclose the religious or communal motivations behind their vote choice. But even while assuming that religious polarization was an important driver of the Hindu vote consolidation, the dilution of clear caste-based voting is still striking, given that scholars believe that caste calculations are most salient and defined in north India.

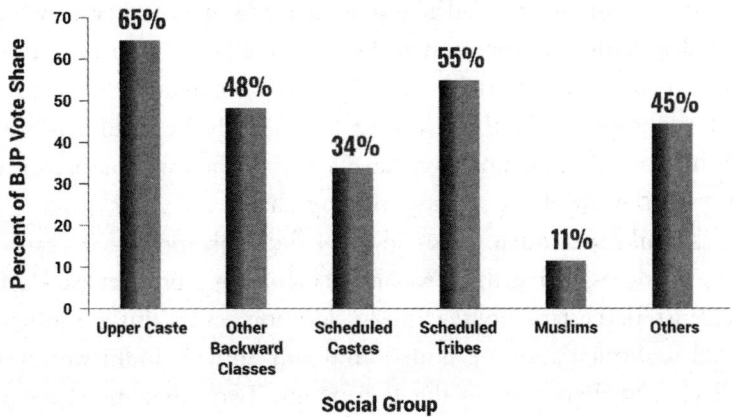

Source: Centre for the Study of Developing Societies, India National Election Study 2014

Clearly, caste as a useful social factor for political mobilization is by no means dead (as is evident from the 2015 Bihar election). However, there are incipient signs that the influence caste once commanded may now be waning. In the 2014 election, there was a clear shift in the performance of key regional parties, which can be attributed to caste. 'Regionally located' parties performed far worse than 'regionalist' parties, the key difference being that the former are typically motivated by underlying caste and community considerations, while the latter represent the interests of a particular state, regional culture or language.

Indeed, the top performing regional parties in 2014—All India Anna Dravida Munnetra Kazhagam (AIADMK), the Trinamool Congress and the Biju Janata Dal (BJD)—which collectively won 91 seats, all conform to the 'regionalist' concept.

When it comes to the Indian voter in 2014, however, there is a mixed picture. It is clear that there are important changes going on, necessitating at least a revision, if not a full-scale replacement of many commonly held notions. While the 2014 election was a watershed moment in Indian politics in terms of its outcome, many of the changes it appeared to herald were actually in operation well before the landmark poll. Nuanced changes in the nature of economic and ethnic voting had already been under way. What the 2014 election may have accomplished was perhaps the crystallization of the already existing changes.

While the Indian voter in 2014 did look mobilized against the Congress party, there was no evidence of a broader backlash against hereditary politicians. In addition, even this sentiment had its limits; after all, both Rahul and Sonia Gandhi were re-elected to their seats in the Parliament. Two other members of the extended family, Maneka Gandhi and her son Varun won the re-election on BJP tickets. With regard to politicians implicated in criminal activities, the 2014 result shows that the nexus of crime and politics was more entrenched than ever. And the rise of regional parties demonstrated that, although they remain key power brokers in Indian politics, there is nothing linear or preordained about their rise.

More broadly, the 2014 election reveals much about the state of India's democracy. First, while voters may harbour deep-seated social biases, political appeals based on identity grounds rarely seem effective on their own to today's Indian voter. In 2014, the BJP managed to forge a genuine cross-caste political coalition that proved to be electoral dynamite. Sceptics rightly point out that such inter-caste bonhomie was only possible because of the BJP's appeal to Hindu nationalism, which polarized the votes of Hindus (in favour of the BJP) and Muslims (largely against the party, given that 8.5 per cent of the community voted for the BJP). While Hindu nationalism did have a role to play in the campaign, it alone was not powerful enough to create a pan-Indian appeal for the BJP. Religious solidarity had to be paired with the promise of governance and development.

On this count, it is encouraging to see voters demonstrating an increased propensity to consider broad indicators of the government's performance in managing the economy when making electoral calculations. This is a positive development when viewed through the prism of governance and democratic accountability. For the moment, identity-based concerns and economic or programmatic evaluations are both in play. Politicians who seek to gain strength on the basis of identity-based appeals alone have generally experienced hard times. The politicians who have fared better have found credible ways of integrating traditional appeals on the basis of identity with a forward-looking aspirational agenda.

It is striking that while the motivations of voters might be shifting, the make-up of the candidate pool they have to choose from is stagnant. In some sense, voters have more choice than ever before, as evidenced by the increase in the number of parties contesting the elections. Yet, there is some qualitative change in the nature of candidates themselves. Dynastic politicians and those with criminal records remain well ensconced in state and national politics. Furthermore, politics continues to be a heavily male-dominated affair. In 1957, the first general election for which data on gender is available, only 3 per cent women contested, out of which only 4.5 per cent made it to the Parliament. While those numbers have gradually increased—in 2014, women accounted for 8.1 per cent of the overall candidate pool and 11.2 per cent of the winners—women remain massively underrepresented in the Parliament, relative to their ratio in the general population.

While the overall balance of power between regional and national parties seems to have reached a steady equilibrium, the fortunes of the Congress and the BJP have seen significant shifts. For the first four decades of the post-Independence period, the Congress was the axis around which Indian politics was organized, which changed significantly after the landmark election of 1989, which paved the way for coalition politics when there was no clear centre of gravity in national politics.

By virtue of its performance in the 2014 general election, and the state assembly elections held before and after the national poll, the BJP has strongly registered its presence at the centre and many states at the expense of the Congress, which received its worst score since Independence in the Parliament. Looking at the continued decline of the Congress, it is difficult to foresee whether this shift is temporary or whether it will continue over time.

In some ways, from the BJP's perspective, this changing of the guard is both a blessing and a curse. In states where the BJP and the Congress are the only contenders, the Congress party's loss will automatically be the BJP's gain. However, the situation is more complex in states where the BJP and the Congress are vying for space with one or more regional parties. In these states, such as Bihar and West Bengal, a rapid decline of the Congress could lead to the consolidation of an anti-BJP front, especially if the Congress avoids contesting elections on its own and develops new regional allies. As the BJP might soon learn, this is one of the unfortunate consequences of being the pole around which politics is organized.

In the 2014 election, the upper middle class and the middle class made all the difference. So let us look at:

How the upper middle class and middle class voted

A significant difference between the 2009 and the 2014 elections was the voter turnout of the upper middle class and the middle class, in terms of their higher population proportion. The total vote constituted by these two classes rose from 26 per cent to 47 per cent in 2009 (Table 1). In terms of the overall turnout, there was an increase from 58 per cent to 68 per cent (Table 2). This is partly due to the definitional effect of the cut-offs for class definitions remaining the same and hence for a much larger percentage of the sample falling in these two classes. Interestingly, the turnout by the poor, at 60 per cent, was significantly lower than the 68 per cent turnout by the two richer classes (Table 2). This pattern was similar to that in Western countries, where those who were economically better off in society and more educated turned out in higher numbers than the poor. The turnout of the upper middle class and the middle class was equal to that of the lower class and much higher than the poor class, regardless of rural, town/city or metropolitan location (Table 3), except for the upper middle class in towns/cities compared to the lower class (but still higher than the poor).

Table 1: Class Composition in 2009 and 2014

Class	2009	2014
Poor	41	20
Lower	33	33
Middle	20	36
Upper	6	11

Source: Centre for the Study of Developing Societies, India National Election Study 2014

Table 2: Class-Wise Turnout in 2009 and 2014

Class	Voter Turnout	
	2009	2014
Poor	57	60
Lower	59	68
Middle	60	69
Upper	57	67
Total	58	67

Source: Centre for the Study of Developing Societies, India National Election Study 2014

Table 3: Class-Wise Voter Turnout in Rural-Urban Locations

Class	Congress 2009–2014		BJP 2009–2014		Metro 2009–2014	
Poor	58	63	56	57	44	50
Lower	60	70	60	64	50	56
Middle	61	71	59	66	52	57
Upper	59	71	53	59	57	69
Total	59	69	58	63	49	57

Source: Centre for the Study of Developing Societies, India National Election Study 2014

Also, a larger proportion of metropolitan votes compared to 2009 were accounted for by the upper middle and the middle classes due to their higher turnout and higher proportion in the electorate. The higher turnout by the upper middle and middle classes in metros could be the sign of a new trend, as India urbanizes rapidly and as the middle classes, holding cut-offs constant, grows in relative size. Analysts believe that as the upper middle and the middle classes are disproportionately upper-caste, it could be a windfall for the Right-wing BJP (36 per cent and 25 per cent, respectively).

Of the total pro-BJP vote in the sixteenth parliamentary election, 52 per cent came from the top two classes (Table 4). The age group within classes does not seem to have made a big overall difference, but it is noteworthy that first-time voters (40 per cent pro-BJP in the middle class) and the under-35 age group in the upper middle class (Table 5) were disproportionately pro-BJP. This younger age group's relatively greater orientation towards the BJP could possibly be a sign of things to come, as this generation rises and the older generations fades out.

Table 4: Class-Wise Party Preference

Class	Congress 2009–2014		BJP 2009–2014	
Poor	27	20	16	24
Lower	29	19	19	31
Middle	29	20	22	32
Upper	29	17	25	38
Total	29	19	19	31

Source: Centre for the Study of Developing Societies, India National Election Study 2014

Table 5: Party Preference of Voters by Different Class and Age Groups

Age Group	Poor		Lower		Middle		Upper	
	Congress	BJP	Congress	BJP	Congress	BJP	Congress	BJP
18–22	23	24	18	35	17	40	11	44
23–25	24	25	18	34	21	32	16	43
26–35	19	27	21	33	19	33	17	40
36–45	18	24	17	30	20	32	15	36
46–55	19	22	21	31	20	31	20	35
56 and above	20	22	18	28	23	29	21	35
Total	20	24	19	31	20	32	17	38

Source: Centre for the Study of Developing Societies, India National Election Study 2014

The upper-middle-class and middle-class preference for the BJP (38 per cent and 32 per cent, respectively) was more marked than that of the rest of the sample, being 31 per cent for lower and only 24 per cent for the poor (Table 4), and this is still more marked in the case of the upper-caste component of these two classes (46 per cent middle-class and 55 per cent upper-middle-class pro-BJP [Table 6]). While in 2009, the BJP overtook the Congress only in the upper castes (36 per cent to 26 per cent [Table 6]), in 2014 it led the Congress in all castes/communities, except Muslims and Christians, but particularly among the upper castes (Table 6). Therefore, data shows a strong affinity for the BJP among the upper middle and the middle classes, and among the upper castes, who have a disproportionately high share in these classes, as well as the younger age groups among the upper middle and the middle classes. Among the upper middle class in the metros, there is a seeming emergence of the loose 'new social bloc' of economic and social privilege after fifteen years of high growth, rising incomes and greater urbanization by historical standards. This also seems to fit with the top-middle affinity postulated by Iversen and Soskice for majoritarian electoral systems without a corporatist organization of the economy. The key questions remain in explaining the upper- and middle-class shift towards the BJP.

Table 6: Party Preference of Voters by Different Classes and Caste/Community

Caste/Community	Poor		Lower		Middle		Upper	
	Congress	BJP	Congress	BJP	Congress	BJP	Congress	BJP
Upper caste	13	37	11	48	15	46	13	55
OBC	15	28	15	37	16	33	14	37
SC	17	22	18	22	20	27	17	25
ST	28	33	31	36	25	39	26	53
Muslims	41	4	34	10	42	11	27	7
Others	19	17	23	18	22	24	31	16
Total	20	24	19	31	20	32	17	38

Source: Centre for the Study of Developing Societies, India National Election Study 2014

After assembly elections in five states in March 2017, sociologist and former professor at JNU Dipankar Gupta, in an op-ed, commented, 'In the past, conventional wisdom believed that the majority community would be equally divided and hence the trick was to win the minority to tip the scales. In recent times, and in the most recent elections in India, this formula lies dead in the water.'[21] A look at the analysis reveals that in constituencies with over 25 per cent Muslim voters, the BJP won 57 seats, while the SP-Congress combine and the BSP put together won only 28 and 3 seats, respectively. So what worked for the BJP was majority consolidation and not minority fine-tuning. As Gupta puts it, 'The fight from now on is not "my minority versus yours", but "my majority versus yours".'[22] Well-known editor and a former minister in the BJP government, M.J. Akbar, felt that Muslims voted for the BJP because they relied on facts. To quote Akbar, 'Muslims can see for themselves that Mudra loans or insurance or LPG are as available to them as anyone else on the basis of poverty and not faith.'[23]

But why did the upper middle and the middle classes vote for the BJP disproportionately in 2014? After all, this was not the pattern after five years of high growth under the UPA-I in 2009. So it cannot be assumed that the growth of the upper middle and the middle classes automatically translates into pro-BJP preferences. The key questions that remain are:

- Was it due to an anti-minority sentiment promoted as an undercurrent by the BJP campaign, at least in certain states such as UP?
- Was it due to a Rightward shift in views among the population on economic policy issues?
- Was it due to the upper middle and the middle classes' dissatisfaction with their economic condition, and was the upper-middle and the middle-class shift towards the BJP part of Hindu consolidation on an anti-minority platform?
- Was there an attitudinal shift towards economic liberalization on the whole?

While the reasons are still unclear behind this preference, it can be inferred that the Congress's anti-poverty programmes and employment-guarantee programmes did not catch the popular imagination as they apparently did in 2009.

Various post-election analyses show that neither Hindu majoritarianism nor dissatisfaction with the movement in their economic condition over the past five years explains the pro-BJP swing.

One can only speculate that there was a general dissatisfaction among the upper middle and middle classes with their current economic condition, compared to what seemed to be heightened expectations and aspirations.

So was it finally the BJP/Modi campaign?

Discontent of the middle class, along with Modi's charismatic persona, seemed to credibly promise the energetic Modi campaign, which included his untiring reaching out to millions of people, as compared to the lacklustre Congress campaign. The low ratings of the Congress leadership, compared to Modi's, in response to questions such as who the respondents preferred as the prime minister, picked up by Lokniti and other tracker polls since Modi was projected as the BJP's prime ministerial candidate since September 2013, backed this up.

There was some support for the Modi factor, in that as many as 23 per cent of the upper middle and middle classes said they would have voted for a different party had Modi not been the BJP candidate, although this was not limited to pro-BJP/National Democratic Alliance (NDA) voters.

On the whole, one can say that, in 2014, the class-wise gradation of pro-BJP responses, with pro-BJP sentiment rising as we go up the class and caste hierarchy, indicate support for the emergence of a loose, not compact, 'new social bloc' of class and caste privilege. This supports the Iversen-Soskice finding (2006) that majoritarian electoral systems tend towards a top-middle alliance in the absence of a corporatist economic structure.

Author E. Sridharan argues that the attitude of the Indian middle classes towards liberalization is complex and contradictory, because a large fraction of the middle class, though declining gradually over time with the growth of the private sector and also as we go up the class hierarchy, are public employees broadly defined.[24]

Thus, an estimated 58–75 per cent of the broadest middle class of 26 per cent of the population, as of the turn of the century, were either public employees or (publicly subsidized) rich peasants; and even of the elite middle class of 6 per cent, as of 2005–06, as many as 30 per cent belonged to these segments.[25]

Even those of the middle classes who are self-employed or private employees are, like public employees or rich peasants, the beneficiaries of a range of state subsidies, including water, electricity, fertilizer, credit, fuel, higher education, public transport and even food (which is supposed to go to the truly poor). In India, subsidies are not simply benefits paid to the poor out of taxes paid by the rich, as the debate is framed in developed democracies, particularly by the Right. The upper and middle classes, as defined in the National Election Study (NES), account for 48 per cent of the population in 2014, who cannot all be counted as part of a privileged group. Economic liberalization that rolls back the role of the state would threaten the jobs of both public and private employees, subsidy-dependent rich peasants and other members of the middle classes, and that is why one can expect to see the ambivalence or complexity of the responses to liberalization noted above.

Hence, one can expect the middle classes' political alignments to be complexly determined by competition for patronage interwoven with identity politics, party loyalties and ideology.

Besides, the poorer classes and lower castes also voted for the BJP over the Congress or any other party in this election, a factor that needs explanation and one that cannot be explained in terms of redistributive programmes or patronage politics, except, perhaps, in the limited number of BJP-ruled states.

Class was, therefore, only one of several axes of polarization in India in 2014, and class politics—in the sense of developed democracies, particularly in Europe, or the Left-Right axis on economic policy as in those countries—was still not the norm in India.

Overall, given the extremely regionally skewed nature of the BJP victory—with 244 seats of its 282 coming from the Hindi-belt states and western India, accounting for only 61 per cent of the population—we need to have regionally disagreeable survey data to be able to fully comprehend the voting trends by class, caste/community and age groups within each region, as well as the attitudes towards minorities and majoritarianism, and towards economic policy questions, which we do not have as of now.

To sum up, it is too early to be able to confidently project the trends in this election into the future. However, what one can be sure of is that the campaign—and the manner in which Modi was projected in 2014 and the elections fought—remains the mother of all elections so far and has set the trend for future political campaigns and the way elections will be fought from now on. The campaigning style, strategies and the resounding victory in the UP assembly election in April 2017 has only vindicated this.

Notes

1. Mahapatra, Dhananjay, and Choudhary, Amit A., "SC: Candidate Using Religion, Caste, Race, Community to Seek Votes Can Be Debarred", *The Times of India*, 3 January 2017, p.1, p.10
2. http://www.elections.in/political-corner/universal-adult-suffrage/
3. Ibid
4. Mishra, Asit R., Anuja, Tandon, Suneera, and Verma, Gyan, "Census Profiles the Young Indian Voter, Spender", LiveMint, 7 September 2013

http://www.livemint.com/Politics/B1tnK7YhZZUYb56bLJL9kK/Census-profiles-the-young-Indian-voter-spender.html
5. http://www.indexmundi.com/india/demographics_profile.html
6. Flanigan, William H., and Zingale, Nancy N., *Political Behavior of the American Electorate,* CQ Press, Washington, 1994, pp.33–35
7. Campbell, Angus, et al, *Elections and the Political Order,* John Wiley & Sons, New York, 1966, pp.40–62
8. Ibid
9. Tripathi, Rahul, "The Motivation to Vote", *The Times of India,* 3 March 2012
https://timesofindia.indiatimes.com/city/goa/The-motivation-to-vote/articleshow/12116919.cms
10. "Over 1,900 Parties in India, 400 Never Fought Polls: EC", *The Times of India,* 8 December 2016
https://timesofindia.indiatimes.com/india/Over-1900-parties-in-India-400-never-fought-polls-EC/articleshow/55862938.cms
11. "PM Narendra Modi Is World No.3 on Twitter, No.1 on Facebook, Instagram", Livemint, 11 July 2018
https://www.livemint.com/Politics/d9msMK13chc6bwTFyWkMNO/PM-Narendra-Modi-is-world-No-3-on-Twitter-No1-on-Facebook.html
12. The CII Big Picture Summit was organized by the Confederation of Indian Industry (CII) at the Taj Hotel in New Delhi from 19 October to 20 October 2015
13. https://www.sri.com/sites/default/timeline/timeline.php?timeline=business-entertainment#!&innovation=vals-market-research
14. Vaishnav, Milan, "Understanding the Indian Voter", Carnegie Endowment for International Peace
https://carnegieendowment.org/files/understanding_indian_voter.pdf
15. Kalra, Neha, "Tata Tea: Jaago Re to Corruption", afaqs!, 26 August 2009
http://www.afaqs.com/news/story/24780_Tata-Tea-Jaago-Re-to-Corruption

16. Baran, Stanley J., and Davis, Dennis K., *Mass Communication Theory: Foundations, Ferment, and Future*, Wadsworth Publishing, pp.125–145
17. Desai, Santosh, "The Mystery of the Invisible Wave?", in his column "City City Bang Bang", *The Times of India*, 13 March 2017 https://timesofindia.indiatimes.com/blogs/Citycitybangbang/the-mystery-of-the-invisible-wave/
18. Chauhan, Chanchal, "AAP Complains to EC About Alleged EVM Tampering in Punjab Elections, Submits Evidence", India.com, 28 March 2017 http://www.india.com/news/india/aap-complains-to-ec-about-allegedevm-tampering-in-punjab-elections-submits-evidence-1969140/
19. Ibid
20. Srivastava, Kanchan, "EVM-Paper Trail Introduced in 8 of 543 Constituencies", *DNA*, 27 April 2014 http://www.dnaindia.com/mumbai/report-evm-paper-trailintroduced-in-8-of-543-constituencies-1982463
21. Gupta, Dipankar, "Lesson of 2017: Decisive Leadership Wins Elections", *The Times of India*, 12 March 2017
22. Ibid
23. Akbar, M.J., "The Poor Have Embraced Modi, and the Vote-Merchants Still Don't Get It", *The Times of India*, 12 March 2017
24. Sridharan, E., "Middle-Class Votes For BJP", *Electoral Politics in India: The Resurgence of the Bharatiya Janata Party*, eds. Suhas Palsikar et al, Routledge, New York, 2017
25. Ibid

5

IDEAS, IDEOLOGIES AND CAMPAIGN PLANKS: DECONSTRUCTING ELECTION CAMPAIGNS 1984–2014

> 'Give me the liberty to know, to utter and to argue freely according to conscience, above all liberties.'
>
> —JOHN STUART MILL

Seventy years is not a long time in the making of a nation. India, which the world often referred to as a fledgling democracy, has shown that though it may have a long way to go to conquer its myriad problems, such as poverty and social equity, it has a robust democratic ethos and value system, if the last sixteen general elections and many hundred state-level elections of the past seven decades are any indication.

Election times verily reflect the mood of a nation, and it is not uncommon to see it reflected in the slogans coined by various political parties, either to score a point or to deride an opponent. High-decibel campaigns, riding on rhetoric and creating perceptions, are commonplace during election times.

One of the greatest political philosophers of all time, Aristotle, identified three principle modes of rhetoric—deliberative, forensic and demonstrative—in political communication. The deliberative rhetoric is designed to sway people on matters of public policy by deliberating on the relative advantages and disadvantages of the alternative way of things. Its focus is on what will happen in future, given the proposed policies. It is expected to create and modify expectations to come. The forensic rhetoric focuses on what has happened in the past in order to demonstrate guilt and innocence, responsibility, or punishment and reward. Its normal setting is the courtroom, but it can occur anywhere, especially in political communication during elections. The demonstrative rhetoric is a discourse of praise and blame. Its intent is to amplify the good and bad qualities of a person, institution or idea. Political campaigns are generally replete with demonstrative rhetoric, as opponents challenge each other's qualifications for the public office. For instance, taking a leaf from the 2014 campaign, from the respectful NaMo versus RaGa to the not-so-respectful Fenku versus Pappu, there were well-thought-out sobriquets and jibes against both Modi and Rahul Gandhi by both the parties. The Congress called Modi *'maut ka saudagar'* (trader of death), and Modi mockingly referred to Rahul Gandhi as 'shehzada' (prince).

It is not uncommon at such times to find the media creating narratives around various actors, amplifying the positive qualities of some candidates and the negative qualities of others through editorials, opinionated articles, reportage and news programmes, thus serving the electorate a menu card to choose from.

Campaigning in earlier times

In the following paragraphs, we shall deconstruct select campaigns between 1984 and 2014 to see their content and positioning planks. But first, the state of campaigning in earlier times.

India had its first general election in 1952. Before independent India went for its maiden polls, two former cabinet colleagues of Pandit Jawaharlal Nehru established separate political parties—

Shyama Prasad Mookerjee founded the Jana Sangh in October 1951 and Dr Ambedkar revived the Scheduled Castes Federation (which was later named the Republican Party). A number of other political parties, such as the Kisan Mazdoor Praja Parishad by Acharya Kripalani, the Congress Socialist Party by Ram Manohar Lohia and Jayaprakash Narayan, and the CPI were also founded. They all fought the election to register their ideological stand, irrespective of whether they expected success in their first electoral battle. Nehru became the first elected prime minister of the country, his party beating rivals by winning 75.99 per cent (47,665,951) of the votes cast.[1]

All elections are fought on ideas, ideologies and interests. The more the competition, the more the need for positioning a party or a candidate vis-à-vis the competition and the prevailing environment. Socioeconomic and political scenarios, both actual and 'created' by rivals and reinforced by the media stimuli, generally steer support towards or away from the incumbent government and other contenders. To quote an instance, about a year short of the sixteenth parliamentary election, 'policy paralysis' to describe the state of the UPA government caught the imagination of the media in its discussions and reportage. This became the talking point in the campaigns of the contending parties. Social media had its share of jokes and slurs on the alleged policy paralysis and the 'silent' prime minister. It seemed the Congress top leadership and party workers had given up even before a fight.

After a quarter-century of uninterrupted power from 1952 to 1977, the Congress party—initially formed as the Indian National Congress, and later Congress (I)—faced an unprecedented defeat in 1977, such that even Indira Gandhi, the then prime minister, lost her election deposit, an electoral punishment for imposing 'Internal Emergency' on the country, that took away many civil rights of the common man. This, in a way, was the first real triumph of the electoral democracy in the country.

The 1977 general election has often been described as a watershed moment in Indian democracy, as, for the first time, a non-Congress government, which was a coalition of sorts, called the Janata Party, took the reins of power. However, held two years later, they were beaten in the next election and the Congress was back in power. This reflected the inherent power of the Indian electorate, which asserted its decision both times within this short interval. The period between 1984 and 2014 saw the step-by-step ascent of the BJP, to the extent that, in 2014, the Congress suffered its worst defeat by winning only 70 seats in a house of 540 in the sixteenth parliamentary election. This period also saw the entry of marketing agencies, opinion pollsters and top-notch advertising agencies strategizing party campaigns, as they would for brands. Many analysts felt that it was, in a way, the Americanization of elections in this part of the world.

Campaigning in earlier times

With practically no mass media except the press on the scene during the 1952 election, parties used door-to-door canvassing, rallies and outdoor media, including posters, buntings, party flags and wall paintings to reach out to voters. It was commonplace until the 1970s to give party symbols as trinkets during door-to-door canvassing. Made from plastic, the oxen pair in tricolour from the Congress and the orange-coloured lamp from the erstwhile Jana Sangh were very popular trinkets with party workers and children.

Historian Ramachandra Guha in his book *India After Gandhi* has mentioned that one could see 'Vote Congress' painted on cows on the streets of Calcutta (now Kolkata). There were no catchy slogans per se during the first couple of elections after India became independent.

It is believed that P.K. Atre, a journalist from Maharashtra, was the first to coin a slogan in the context of the first general election, albeit after the results were announced, when Dr Ambedkar conceded defeat to an unknown butter-seller, Narayan Sadoba Kajrolkar. The Marathi slogan Atre came up with read: '*Kuthe to ghatnakar Ambedkar, aani kuthe ha lonivikya Kajrolkar?*' This meant, 'Where is the great Constitution-maker, Ambedkar, and where is the obscure butter-seller, Kajrolkar?'

Analysts believe that there was no curbing of funny, whacky or sarcastic slogans in future elections. The Jana Sangh, a Rightwing party, can be credited for starting the slogan war, using at times unheard-of insinuations and cuss words in them. Others such as the Congress and the regional parties also did not lag behind in trading charges, many times unfounded. To quote a few instances, during the 1967 election, the Jana Sangh used the slogan: '*Jana Sangh ko vote do, bidi peena chhod do; bidi mein tambaku hai, Congress-wala daaku hai.*' This roughly translated to: 'Vote for the Jana Sangh and stop smoking; just as the cigarette has tobacco, a Congressman is a plunderer.' Though the two parts of the sentence were unconnected, the slogan rhymed well and caught the attention of the voters, asking them to reject both the Congress and tobacco with a single slogan.

The Sixties was a period of ordeal for the common man. The population was increasing disproportionately to the country's resources, forcing the government to import foodgrains. With there being no electricity in most parts of the country, kerosene was also in short supply. People got sugar, kerosene and foodgrains as ration. Long queues could be seen outside authorized ration shops. The Jana Sangh had another innovative slogan to deride the Congress party, who, after the demise of Nehru, put forward Indira Gandhi as the prime minister. The slogan was: '*Yeh dekho Indira ka khel, kha gayi shakkar, pee gayi tel.*' This meant, 'Look at the game Indira is playing; she has eaten all the sugar and guzzled all the kerosene.' The Jana Sangh's election campaign highlighted the state of inflation during the Congress government's tenure.

The Congress presented itself as the face of development and launched the Progress Through Congress campaign in the 1960s.

When Indira Gandhi split the Congress party to form the Congress (I), her reply to the Syndicate's[2] *'Indira hatao'* was *'Yeh kahate hein Indira hatao, mein kehti hoon garibi hatao.'* This meant, 'They say "remove Indira", I say remove poverty.' This became a slogan for the election, positioning her strongly against the Syndicate. The 'I' in the bracket could mean Indira as well as India. The liberation of Bangladesh in 1971 gave a larger-than-life persona to her. Her party never shied away from claiming that 'India was Indira and Indira was India'. She was even seen as the personification of Goddess Durga by some after the liberation of Bangladesh.

Just a few years later, when her election was challenged by the Allahabad High Court, she declared Emergency in June 1975. Socialist leader Jayaprakash Narayan's Janata Party raised a powerful slogan against Indira Gandhi's campaign post Emergency, with *'Indira hatao, desh bachao'*, which meant 'Remove Indira, save the country'.

After losing the election in 1977, Indira Gandhi contested a by-election in 1978 from Chikmagalur district in Andhra Pradesh. Poet Srikant Verma, in a bid to mock the Opposition for doing precious little in a non-Congress government, coined a funny yet catchy slogan for Indira Gandhi, which read, *'Ek sherni, sau langur, Chikmagalur, bhai, Chikmagalur.'* This can roughly be translated as, 'What are a hundred monkeys when compared to one lioness? This time, it is Chikmagalur, brothers, Chikmagalur.' The place of her contest, Chikmagalur, rhymed well with langur, or monkey.

The Eighties saw the rise of terrorism in Punjab and increased militancy in the state of Jammu and Kashmir. The decision to flush out Bhindranwale and his supporters from the Golden Temple in Amritsar with Operation Blue Star[3] brought unrest within the Sikh community. Indira Gandhi, then prime minister of India, was gunned down at her official residence by two of her Sikh security men on 31 October 1984, as she was coming out to meet a waiting media team for an interview. The mantle of the top job in the country passed to her son, Rajiv Gandhi, immediately thereafter.

The 1984 general election

The assassination of Indira Gandhi was followed by unprecedented riots, resulting in the brutal killing of thousands of innocent Sikhs. A few Congress leaders were alleged to have led the killing, loot and arson of Sikhs and their properties, especially in the capital city of Delhi. Riots erupted elsewhere in the country too, but Delhi was the worst hit. When asked by the media about the killings, the newly appointed prime minster, Rajiv Gandhi, is believed to have said, 'When a big tree falls, the earth shakes', showing a shocking lack of concern and sympathy for the innocent lives lost.[4]

Besides the death of a serving prime minister, the killing of thousands of innocent Sikhs and the issue of Khalistan in Punjab, fanned by Pakistan on the one hand and separatist Sikh elements abroad on the other, the other worrisome reality of the time was the increasing insurgency in Jammu and Kashmir. Elections were announced soon after Indira Gandhi's death to have the public's mandate.

The 1984 elections can be said to be a watershed in India's campaigning style and strategies. High budgets, the branding of parties and politicians, and the entry of top-notch advertising agencies began with this election.

A reticent Rajiv Gandhi depended on his close friend, Arun Singh, and cousin Arun Nehru, who, it is believed, suggested the name of the ad agency Rediffusion for the top job, with Arun Nanda, the proprietor, himself taking the brief with his team from the prime minister.

The 1984 campaign of the Congress (I) used fear as a strategy.

One of the ads showed a barbed wire, signifying the Indian border. The headline read: 'Will the country's border finally be moved to your doorstep?' The subhead read: 'India could be a vote away. From unity to separatism.' The tagline of the campaign was, 'Give unity a hand.' The hand, which is the symbol of the Congress party, was used as a metaphor. Another ad had the headline, 'Will your grocery list in future include acid bulbs, iron rods and daggers?', with the subhead, 'India could be a vote away from order to chaos; give order a hand'.

The Congress received an unprecedented mandate across the country. The party garnered more than 400 seats, equivalent to three-fourth seats in the Parliament, and seemed to be riding the sympathy wave after Indira Gandhi's assassination. The campaign seemed to reinforce the public's faith in the party.

Many years later, Ajit Balakrishnan, one of the team members of Rediffusion that did the Congress campaign (he is now the Chairman and Chief Executive Officer of Rediff.com), posted on his blog the story behind the campaign. The box below is an excerpt:[5]

The Congress Party Ad Campaign for the 1984 Lok Sabha Elections

Rajiv Gandhi had been shanghaied into politics as the general secretary of the Congress party; he had, in turn, shanghaied his friends Arun Singh and Arun Nehru into the party to help improve the party's fast-dwindling chances in the imminent Lok Sabha elections. Arun Singh was at Reckitt & Coleman and Arun Nehru at Jenson & Nicholson, two clients for whom Rediffusion had just done feted ad campaigns. So when our clients were called to Delhi, so were we. The presentation that we were all peering at was making a significant point. India, in the 1980s, had an electorate of several hundred millions, but we had discovered through rigorous computer-based statistical analysis that only a very small percentage determined election outcomes; the balance were loyalists consistently voting for the same party in every successive election. When we ran these numbers on our computers more deeply, we discovered that these swing voters were very different from the rest; they were literate (in a country still swimming in illiteracy) and they were avid newspaper readers (in a country where newspaper penetration was still miniscule). This insight settled our media plan—we would run the Congress campaign only in print.

As for the creative strategy, much of it suggested itself. Look at what was going on just then. President [Ronald] Reagan had just raised the pitch of the Cold War confrontation by announcing his Star Wars missile defence scheme (March 1983), 3,000 Tamils are massacred in a genocide in Sri Lanka, sparking off the Tamil separatist movement (July 1983), Punjab had been on fire all year long and the Indian Army had just been sent in to flush out Sikh militants from the Golden Temple in Amritsar (June 1984), half a million people are out on the streets of Manila protesting Marcos' rule and Ninoy Aquino's assassination (August 2004) ... Confrontation was everywhere! We correctly guessed that, in this era of uncertainty and turmoil, what the newspaper-reading swing voter wanted was the peace and quiet that only a strong and impartial government could provide.

'Will your grocery list, in the future, include acid bulbs, iron rods, daggers?' asked the first ad. Ordinary citizens, we argued, need to arm themselves only when governments become weak. Your vote can make the difference between order and chaos. Vote for the Congress.

'Will the country's border finally move to your doorstep?' asked the next, casting an eye on the raging separatist movements. Would you soon look uneasily at your neighbour, just because he belongs to another community? Vote for the Congress and vote for unity, otherwise it is a vote for separatism.

The campaign was ready to go on four-week notice, as the monsoon of 1984 was drawing to a close. We went back to our day job of trying to make soaps and detergents and toothpaste exciting to consumers, awaiting the start signal from the Congress party.

Then came the bombshell.

On 31 October, two trusted Sikh guards on Mrs Gandhi's security detail (how many times we must have greeted these two while on our way to meetings there) assassinated her. We and the whole country watched in horror as Delhi went up in flames.

Suddenly, the words we had crafted many, many months ago started ringing even truer than when we had written them.

Would we, ordinary, law-abiding citizens, have to now go shopping for acid bulbs, iron rods and daggers to protect our families from the marauding crowds? Would we start looking uneasily at our neighbours because they came from a different community? Would it now become difficult to find an Indian among the millions of Sikhs and Hindus and Punjabis and Tamils and others? Would the country descend into chaos?

Elections were called soon afterwards. The ad campaign ran as it was first created many months before that. In an amazing turn of events, reality had caught with our ad campaign. And this reality, grimmer than we had ever imagined, heightened the nuances of the words and pictures we had used in the ad campaign and gave them an urgency we had not seen when we had created them.

From Balakrishnan's version, it is clear that the campaign with barbed wires and acid bulbs as graphics was not an afterthought to the assassination of Indira Gandhi, but keeping in mind the prevailing conditions not only in India but elsewhere as well. Her death only reinforced the situation the country was in.

It is, however, strange that the public's voting was not influenced by the mass killing of thousands of innocent Sikhs. What could one ascribe this indifference to? Loyalty is an important trait in any individual. The security guards, whose job was to protect the prime minister, ended up becoming her killers—something unexpected and unacceptable on moral grounds and in the call of duty. The cruel vendetta that followed the killing did not seem to matter to the electorate.

Vajpayee, who was then the president of the BJP, according to media reports, had instructed party leaders in Delhi to organize relief camps and provide succour to survivors. Politicians Madan Lal Khurana and Vijay Kumar Malhotra are said to have gone from one colony to another, giving whatever help the party could.[6] However, the public opinion seemed to sway only in favour of the Congress. The BJP managed only two seats in the 1984 Lok Sabha election.

The election in December 1984, after Indira Gandhi was assassinated, had the slogan, *'Jab tak sooraj chand rahega, Indira tera naam rahega.'* This meant, 'Your name shall shine, Indira, as long as there is light in the sun and the moon.'

Harish Khare, a former Political Science professor and senior journalist, recollecting the state of the country at the time of the 1984 election, commented,

> A conservative, Hindu revolution had swept India... The Indian people have entrusted Rajiv Gandhi with safeguarding the country's unity. He wrapped himself in the flag and sold himself as the political heir to Indira Gandhi, whose assassination by two Sikh security guards in October [1984] became synonymous with an assault on the Indian state...

> The Congress party's triumph is frightening, because Rajiv Gandhi depicted the assault on the state as the work of separatist Sikh fundamentalists. His campaign theme of 'unity in danger' deeply touched many Hindus, appealing subtly to their historical fears and mistrust of non-Hindus... Rajiv Gandhi's mandate can be summed up as a triumph of neo-Hinduism. Thousands of chauvinistic Hindus abandoned their traditional champion—Right-wing parties like the Bharatiya Janata Party—to rally under his banner. And though those parties have been decimated, the Right-wing constituency has, in fact, been strengthened and enlarged, putting the liberal, democratic fringe in mortal danger.[7]

While the Congress could not retain this constituency, it became the BJP's gain in the later elections, when it asserted and regained the constituency that ideologically was always theirs.

The 1989 election campaign

As they say, there is nothing permanent in politics. Thanks to the Bofors gun scam, Rajiv Gandhi, who was often referred to as 'Mr Clean', emerged as 'not so clean', after all.

V.P. Singh, one of Rajiv Gandhi's senior cabinet ministers, who was the defence minister then, raised allegations against Gandhi and got dismissed from the cabinet. He started a new political outfit, Jan Morcha, in 1987, to fight against corruption. V.P. Singh, who had been the UP chief minister earlier, had the reputation of being an honest politician. His crusade against corruption, first against industrialists and then within the government on the Bofors deal, made him popular throughout the country. He went on to form the Janata Dal in 1988 by merging Jan Morcha—which was a faction of the Janata Party led by Chandra Shekhar—Lok Dal and Indian Congress (Socialist). He did not stop there but brought regional satraps in the fold by floating a coalition called National Front, bringing the Dravida Munnetra Kazhagam (DMK) from Tamil Nadu, the Telugu Desam Party (TDP) from Andhra Pradesh and the Asom Gana Parishad from Assam to fight the election together. The election proved to be a disaster for the Congress, as it could not muster a majority, despite being the largest party. Rajiv Gandhi preferred not to stake a claim. It was a windfall for the BJP, which had scored only two seats in the 1984 election, but managed to garner 85 seats in the 1989 election. Its campaign and a parallel surrogate campaign by the Vishva Hindu Parishad (VHP) positioned the party as the Hindu voice that needed to be heard. '*Bachcha bachcha Ram ka, Janmabhoomi ke kaam ka*', meaning 'every child is Ram's and they owe it to Ram Janmabhoomi', was coined as the VHP slogan.

Before the election, the Congress government reduced the voting age from 21 years to 18 years. Analysts believe this was done to create a larger vote base of young people, which the party wrongly thought would go in its favour, as it expected the younger generation to be attracted to the young prime minister and be ignorant of the narrative of corruption against it. This gamble cost the party dearly. The Congress's loss turned out to be the BJP's gain, as with its cadre-based disciplined workforce, it managed to reach out to the school-going population and fresh school passouts through its shakhas and other outreach programmes. It is interesting to find that the Congress, led by Rajiv Gandhi, despite the hard-hitting campaign by the Opposition parties, managed to secure 197 seats, the highest among all parties, with a vote share of a little over 39 per cent. In retrospect, the party had won 405 seats in 1984, with a vote share of over 49 per cent. There was a loss of just 10 per cent in the vote share, but 205 seats.

The Janata Dal, led by V.P. Singh, became the second-largest party, securing 143 seats and a vote share of 40.7 per cent. Left parties secured 45 seats, with a vote share of 9.1 per cent.

The BJP, which had two seats in the eighth Lok Sabha, improved its position and secured 85 seats in 1989, with a vote share of just 11.36 per cent.

The Congress, for its 1989 elections, used the same ad agency as its 1984 campaign. From 'Give unity a hand', Redifussion coined the tagline, 'My heart beats for India', bringing out the theme of Opposition disunity, secessionism and opportunism. The BJP and the National Front, spearheaded by V.P. Singh, had also chiselled their communication weaponry. The media reported that V.P. Singh, in his rallies, would often take out a piece a paper from his pocket in a symbolic gesture to suggest that he had received the name of the prime minister, Rajiv Gandhi, for taking kickbacks from the Bofors sellers. Interestingly, that symbolic chit of paper never surfaced after the election.

From 1989 to 1991, there were two non-Congress governments, the first led by V.P. Singh, which held power for about eleven months, and then by Chandra Shekhar, which held power for four months. The Janata Dal, with many ambitious leaders of different ideologies, could not get along with each other for long. V.P. Singh did not overtly pursue the Bofors inquiry. The economy, which was already under a recessionary spell, worsened. India was seen in the dubious list of debt defaulters. Increased militancy and bloodshed saw about 1 lakh Kashmiri Pandits fleeing from the valley and becoming refugees in their own homeland.

In a bid to consolidate the OBC votes, V.P. Singh, without a wider debate in the Parliament or outside, in August 1990 announced the implementation of the recommendations in the Mandal Commission report, which secured a 27 per cent reservation for admissions and government jobs for the OBC community. This led to widespread agitation by the youth throughout the country, even resulting in the unprecedented self-immolation of dozens of youth against the order. The issue of caste-based reservations has been the cause of a lot of agitation and chaos in the country for over a quarter of a century, since the implementation of the Mandal Commission recommendations. The most recent of such protests was the 2016 Jat agitation in Haryana, which resulted in the destruction of government and private property worth crores by rioters and the alleged sexual assault of several women stranded on the highway.[8]

As if the chaos created by the Mandal implementation was not enough, the BJP announced a rath yatra (journey on a chariot) from Somnath to Ayodhya in a bid to consolidate the Hindu vote. BJP senior leader L.K. Advani started his yatra from Somnath on 20 September 1990, with the aim to reach Ayodhya on 30 October 1990. When beginning his journey, he warned V.P. Singh to not dare curtail his yatra, else his party would withdraw support from the government. Apprehending the law and order situation, the then Bihar chief minister Lalu Prasad Yadav's government issued the order to arrest Advani at Samastipur on 23 October 1990, thus instigating the BJP to withdraw support from the V.P. Singh government at the centre. The government lost the vote of confidence in the Lok Sabha that year on 7 November. Chandra Shekhar and Devi Lal, with sixty-four members, broke away from the Janata Dal and formed the SP. With support from the Congress, Chandra Shekhar became the prime minister of India on 10 November 1990. In just four months' time, on 26 March 1991, the Congress party withdrew its support from the government on the allegation of surveillance on Rajiv Gandhi by two constables. Chandra Shekhar continued to be the prime minister until the next election, when the Congress party came back to power and Narasimha Rao was sworn in as the next prime minister, on 21 June 1991. Rajiv Gandhi, in the meantime, was brutally assassinated during his election campaigning, on 21 May 1991, at Sriperumbudur in Tamil Nadu. The election was halted midway. The poll results did not give majority verdict to the Congress. About 56 per cent of the electorate participated in the polling, giving 244 seats to the Congress, 120 to the BJP, 14 to the CPI and one to the Indian Congress (Socialist). Elections in Punjab and Jammu and Kashmir were not held in 1992. As no party received a majority, the Congress, with support from the CPI, formed the government and went on to have a full term of five years, with Narasimha Rao as the prime minister.

The 1991 election campaign

The political environment, when the elections were announced, was one of confusion—the incumbent prime minister, Chandra Shekhar, had just four months' experience; V.P. Singh had messed up with the reservation issue; and the Congress hoped that people would give it the mandate after having witnessed the state of governance at the hands of coalitions run by V.P. Singh and Chandra Shekhar. Rajiv Gandhi went on his whirlwind election tours, with no respite.

The government allowed free time to all recognized political parties on DD and the AIR to present their views and broadcast political programmes for the audience. The methodology the ECI followed, on 22 April 1991, was through a draw of lots in the presence of representatives of various national political parties. The BJP was the first party to begin the series of broadcasts on 6 May 1991, at 8.20 p.m., on DD. The duration of the programme was fifteen minutes. On the AIR too, all recognized parties were allowed broadcast time in two rounds.[9]

The incumbent prime minister Chandra Shekhar's slogan for the 1991 election—'*Chaar mahine badnaam chalees saal*', which meant 'four months vis-à-vis forty years', exhorting the voters to compare his four months to the forty years of the Congress government—seemed a hollow slogan, as there was nothing much that happened during his tenure.

The Congress repeated the same agency, Redifussion, which

suggested the same plank as in the 1989 election—stability and unity of the country. The strategy and tactics, however, were slightly changed. The tagline this time was, 'Vote Stability. Vote Congress (I).' Common men and women were used as the protagonists of the campaign. In one of the press ads, a young woman clutching her child said, 'I want stability. I want my child safe.' In another ad, the visual showed a Muslim tailor, who said, 'I want my family's life and property secure.' To cover all segments of society, one of the ads had a sarpanch saying, 'I want funds for my panchayat. I want autonomy.' The campaign was adapted in a number of Indian languages to cater to the country's linguistic diversity. The campaign was positive for the urban audience, without any dig taken at any political party. But for the hinterland and the regional-language audience, especially the Hindi heartland, the campaign was hard-hitting and satirical, poking fun at the 'raja', V.P. Singh, who was the adopted son of a king and was married to a princess.

As a strategy, caricatures and well-known proverbs were used. To cite a few examples, one of the ads had the headline, '*Andher nagari, chaupat raja*', which roughly meant, 'In a dark country, the king sleeps'. The visual had a king dozing off on his throne. The headline of another ad was, '*Nau din chale adai kos*', which meant, 'It takes them nine days to drag a mile'. The visual was of a hand cart being pulled in various directions, signifying parties with different ideologies getting together to form the government. A third ad said, '*Kangali mein atta geela*', which meant, 'In poverty, everything turns adverse'. Commenting on Opposition unity, yet another ad had the headline, '*Kahin ki itt, kahin ka gaara, Bhanumati ne kunba joda*', which meant, 'Dissimilar things are being cobbled together to create a semblance of order'. The visual had a misshapen chair under repair. The person perched atop the chair resembled V.P. Singh. High on rhetoric, with a native flavour, the campaign was hard-hitting and critical of the policies of the National Front, headed by V.P. Singh. The incumbent government, led by Chandra Shekhar, was treated with humiliating indifference, as if it were a foregone conclusion that it would not win the 1991 election.

Due to the assassination of the aspiring prime minister Rajiv Gandhi, the Congress changed its strategy in the second phase. The tagline this time was, 'Vote to fulfil Rajiv's dream. Vote Congress (I).' If there was any improvement in the Congress's seats, it was in Phase II, after Rajiv Gandhi's death, but there did not seem to be any sympathy wave this time. The Congress could not muster a majority on its own.

The BJP campaign

The other party that spent significant resources on its campaign was the BJP. In 1989, it projected itself as a non-corrupt party in the face of the Bofors scandal that had mired the Congress's reputation. Having tasted success with 85 seats in 1989, the BJP projected itself as a national alternative to the Congress. The campaign delineated the party's ideology in clear terms and laid out the future course of action to the public. Its headlines were straight and hard-hitting, appealing to a large voter base. One of the headlines was, 'Ramrajya is your birthright.' Another was, 'Freedom from fear.' Yet another was, 'Enough is enough.' Though one felt the undercurrents of Hindutva in its campaign, the party tried to establish its secular credentials. The party also tried to project a cohesive picture of Team BJP, with pictures of all its stalwarts in the same frame wherever possible. Ostensibly separate but integrally intertwined was the VHP's publicity drive to aid and support the BJP campaign. One of the ads was sarcastically headlined 'The wonderful ways of democracy', with the body copy reading, 'Hindus are a majority, divide them. Hindus are peaceful, take them for granted. Hindus are tolerant, dominate them. Hindus oppose violence, rule them. Hindus are awakened, brand them communal. Hindus demand Ram Janmabhoomi, massacre them. Hindus ask for equality, deprive them. Hindus unite, brand them separatist.' The tagline exhorted, 'Hindus unite and act as one. Not against anyone but in defence of our motherland.'

The media in general was openly critical of the VHP campaign. Except for the Congress and the BJP, no other party issued any press advertisements. All other parties, however, brought out audio and video films that were extensively distributed. Popular singers were involved to bring out renditions of myriad political songs. Video vans toured the country, playing these video cassettes. Tempos and scooters could be seen loudly playing political audio cassettes. The outdoor medium had large billboards, kiosks, posters and wall paintings, literally turning the length and breadth of the country into a huge canvas, much to the annoyance of landscape designers and environmentalists. In some research studies conducted, it was seen that the outdoor media ostensibly had the highest recall value.

Communication researcher Bhaskar Rao commented on the 'naivety' and lack of enthusiasm on the part of most parties when using the electronic media. He said, 'Despite the fact that recognized political parties had availed of the electronic media for election-time programmes for the fourth time now [since 1980], most parties gave the impression of using these media for the first time, or perhaps they did not avail them with similar seriousness as they did with video and audio.'[10]

Election manifestos were compared to 'fishing rods' by *The Indian Express*. 'As election manifestos are primarily fishing rods loaded with goodies as baits to catch the susceptible voters, hence the considerable overlap of promises in them,' commented the editorial.[11]

'Hundreds of promises but few ideas,' lamented the editorial of *Business India*. 'The economic content of the manifestos and campaigns of the three major political parties—the Congress, the

National Front and the BJP—bear a striking resemblance to one another.'[12]

In one of the discussions on television, the late S.P. Singh, the editor of the Hindi daily *Navbharat Times*, felt that there was a complete hijacking of the media by the BJP. 'Every time a BJP VIP visited a constituency,' he commented, 'ten to twelve media persons would accompany the caravan, and on return, there obviously would be coverage. An impression was created deliberately by the party through the media messages that "the BJP was sure to sweep the polls".'[13]

Commenting on the sophistication of the marketing armoury employed by the BJP, T.N. Ninan, the editor of *The Economic Times*, said, 'Political campaigns have been like any advertising and marketing plans. Candidates and policies are packaged and marketed most professionally. As market adjustments are made up to keep in view the consumer preference, the BJP did just the same.'[14]

If one were to content-analyse the campaigns of various political parties, it would be evident that the Congress (I) and Samajwadi Janata Party's campaigns revolved around their leaders Rajiv Gandhi and Chandra Shekhar, respectively. The BJP, instead, projected the team.[15]

L.K. Advani, who maintained a low profile during the 1989 election, emerged as the BJP's star candidate for prime ministership during the 1991 election campaign.[16]

The VHP, which had fielded many candidates for the BJP, ran a multiple media campaign simultaneously. The issue was Ram Janmabhoomi and the plank, 'Hindutva'. Though they did not support the party overtly, the informed voter was expected to make the due link. It was, in fact, quite obvious. The BJP received flak for the VHP campaign, which the media commentators termed 'virulent and communal'.[17]

The two major players, who took each other on through their respective campaigns, were the Congress (I) and the BJP. In the

Hindi belt, the Congress (I) targeted the Raja of Manda, V.P. Singh of Janata Dal, who was responsible for the Congress party's defeat in 1989.[18]

The 1996 election campaign

Narasimha Rao's proved to be a landmark government, as it ushered in the era of liberalization of the Indian economy by throwing open its doors to foreign investment in the country. There were two schools of thought prevailing at the time, one that supported and found liberalization inevitable, keeping in view global expectations and the World Bank's insistence on financial reforms, including disinvestment of the public sector; and the other, led by the Swadeshi ideology, which was critical of the government's open policy. Manmohan Singh, a well-known economist, was the finance minister in Rao's cabinet, who later went on to become the prime minister for two terms.

The period witnessed the rise of regional political forces, and alignments and realignments. With smaller parties emerging, the Congress did not seem to have the hold it once did. Advani tried to bring together coalition partners such as the AIADMK and the BSP, but due to ideological differences, the coalitions did not work out. The BJP, however, was able to join with regional parties such as the Samta Party, the Shiv Sena and the Haryana Vikas Party. The Congress tried a regional alliance with the AIADMK. The erstwhile National Front tried to emerge as the 'third force' in the 1996 election, with the Janata Dal, the TDP and the Left Front. It tried to align with many other regional parties, but could not do much. To be able to work against both the Congress and the BJP, the three parties supported the SP in the election. What came out noticeably was that none of the regional parties were ready to align with the national parties.[19]

Just ahead of the election, leaders from across the political spectrum, except from the Left parties, were embroiled in allegations of bribe in what came to be known as the Jain Hawala Case. A bribe of $33 million was said to have been given to various politicians. Some of the prominent names included the late Rajiv Gandhi, Arjun Singh (from the breakaway Congress-T), Sharad Yadav and L.K. Advani. Many were forced to resign. Advani also resigned, paving the way for Vajpayee to be the leader of the Opposition in the Parliament, who later became the prime minister.[20]

The Congress campaign for the 1996 election revolved around its foreign policy record, the handling of various ethnic and natural crises, and concessions to minorities. The campaign bore absolutely no resemblance to the last three high-profile campaigns of the party, which were discussed in the advertising industry and academia for their great finesse. The 1996 campaign posited its anti-communal and secularist stand with the tagline, *'Jaat pe na paat pe, mohar lagegi haath pe.'* The campaign, as mentioned earlier, did not have the sophistication and subtlety of the last few party campaigns.

The BJP's campaign broached various issues, such as probity in public life, social harmony, self-reliance of the economy and greater security. The campaign brought into focus the banning of cow slaughter and its long-time demand for a uniform civil code. The campaign tried to position Vajpayee as the centre of attraction, with the slogan *'Bari bari sab ki bari. Ab ki bari Atal Bihari'*, which meant, 'Everyone will get a chance, but this time it is Atal Bihari's turn'. This rhymed well in Hindi. The Janata Dal and National Front's manifestos also talked about a strong public sector, social equity and subsidy on fertilizers.

No party received a clear verdict in the election. Reacting to the election outcome, *India Today* commented, 'The eleventh Lok Sabha elections saw the eclipse of the National Constituency syndrome that had emerged in the past two decades. Gone are the days when the entire country was like a single constituency which spoke in one, or at the most two, voices to generate the nationwide electoral waves of the '70s and '80s.'[21]

The election saw a massive swing against the Congress, its vote share going down to an all-time low at 30 per cent. The BJP gained by adding 40 more seats without much change in its vote share. The National Front and the Left Front's fortunes remained intact, despite losing the vote share.

Being the largest political party, the BJP was invited to form the government and asked to prove its majority within two weeks. Vajpayee was sworn in as the prime minister on 15 May 1996. When the party could not garner the actual numbers, Vajpayee, instead of facing a vote of confidence on the floor of the house, resigned after thirteen days in tenure, the shortest for any government in the history of parliamentary democracy in India. The second-largest party, the Congress, declined to form the government, and, instead, supported the United Front with H.D. Deve Gowda as the prime minister. With the support of many regional parties and the Congress, Deve Gowda remained the prime minister for less than two years. Internal squabbling and the struggle to maintain balance between diametrically opposed political parties created problems in governance. The Congress offered to support another prime ministerial candidate, the old Congressman I.K. Gujral, to be at the helm of affairs, after ensuring that the government would consult the Congress on various issues and not take unilateral decisions. However, smooth functioning remained elusive for the new dispensation, this time not because of problems from the Congress but from within. The Janata Dal supremo Lalu Prasad Yadav got entangled in the fodder scam. The state governor approved prosecution against him. Gujral advised him to step down, but, at the same time, got Joginder Singh, the Central Bureau of Investigation (CBI) chief who was investigating the fodder scam, transferred, an act that was seen as protecting Yadav.

Realizing that he would not command the same position of power in the Janata Dal, Yadav went ahead and formed the RJD, taking with him seventeen MPs out of forty-five in July 1997. The RJD, however, continued to be part of the coalition. So there was no immediate danger to Gujral's government, which continued for eleven months, including as caretaker prime minister for three months when the polls were announced.

In the 1998 parliamentary election, the BJP again emerged as the largest party, though short of majority. With a coalition called the National Democratic Front, which included the AIADMK, the Trinamool Congress, the SAD, the BSP and the National Conference, the BJP formed the government, with Vajpayee as the prime minister. The NDA lost its majority after AIADMK withdrew its support after the much-talked-about tea party between Rajiv Gandhi's widow, Sonia Gandhi, and the former chief minister of Tamil Nadu, the late J. Jayalalithaa. The president dissolved the Parliament and ordered fresh elections, the third in two years. In the aftermath of the Kargil War and the public's general disdain with smaller parties playing spoilsport, the BJP, with the alliance of major partners DMK and JD(U), received the majority vote and the government continued for a full term of five years until 2004. The NDA comprised a total of twenty-four parties.

The Vajpayee government continued with the liberalization of the economy and disinvestment of the public sector. The first Bhartiya Pravasi Sammelan was organized to take into the fold the Indian diaspora. They were encouraged to invest in India through many measures.

The 1999 election campaign

Things were going badly for the Congress, as its stalwart from Maharashtra, Sharad Pawar, quit the party to make his own—the Nationalist Congress Party—on the issue of Sonia Gandhi's leadership, owing to her foreign roots. This gave a fillip to the BJP, with its theme of 'Videshi versus Swadeshi' (home-grown versus foreign) in its campaign.

The campaigns of both the Congress and the BJP revolved around their leaders, Sonia Gandhi and Vajpayee, respectively. The success of the Kargil War and its apt handling gave the BJP an edge. The Congress's plank was 'single-party rule', reminding the people of the fate of coalition governments in the past three years.

The BJP led the campaign with the slogan *'Jancha, parkha, khara'*, or 'Tried, tested, proven', projecting Vajpayee as its prime ministerial candidate. The campaign used his corruption-free image to attract voters.

Reflecting on the decisive victory of the BJP in the 1999 election, for the first time, the Communist Party of India (Marxist), or the CPI(M), in its review of the election, adopted at its central committee meeting in November 1999, noted,

> The success of the BJP-led alliance in the 1999 Lok Sabha elections, resulting in the return of the Vajpayee government, is a setback for the democratic and secular forces in the country. The CPI(M) had set out the following main tasks to be achieved in the elections: Defeat the BJP alliance, strengthen the Left and democratic representation, and aim for the formation of a secular government at the Centre. The failure to fulfil these aims confirms that the rightward shift in Indian politics continues. We have to properly analyse the election results, assess the present situation and the line of direction of our work.[22]

The 2004 election campaign

The 2004 election was fought between two major coalitions—the NDA, with Vajpayee as the leader, and the UPA, with Sonia Gandhi as the leader.

Winning three assembly elections in a row in 2003—Madhya Pradesh, Chhattisgarh and Rajasthan—gave the BJP the required confidence to ask for an early parliamentary poll to make the most of its gains at the assembly elections. Analysts believe this was a blunder on the part of the party, which, despite doing pretty well on the economic and foreign-policy fronts, mounted the multicrore publicity campaign, India Shining, which proved to be its nemesis. Though things seemed to be going well, the party lost the election.

The general feeling was that the campaign did not find resonance with most Indians, as India was shining in the cities for the rich, but not for the poor in the hinterland. Most media houses and psephologists had predicted victory for the BJP, so the results came as a shock.

Political commentator Guruprasad, in his blog, ascribed the 2004 defeat of the BJP to both the urban and the rural poor, 'who made it a point to "punish" the BJP by voting against it and to bring in the Congress, which was (and has always been) seen as pro-poor. Even L.K. Advani admitted that they lost in 2004 due to overconfidence and wrong slogans like "India Shining".'[23]

Sonia Gandhi, whose foreign roots were an issue in the last election, helped the party sail to victory by making electoral gains with the support of the coalition partners. The Congress focused its campaign on the failures of the NDA government on various fronts and what it had to offer. Facts and figures were used to debunk the government's claims, especially those made through the India Shining campaign. *'Sonia nahi yeh aandhi hai, doosri Indira Gandhi hai'*, which meant, 'This isn't Sonia, this is a storm, she is the next Indira Gandhi', was one of the slogans of the Congress 2004 campaign.[24]

To counter Gandhi's foreign-origin issue, the slogan *'Jan jan ki yehi pukar, Sonia Gandhi bahu hamar'*, meaning, 'In the voice of the common man, Sonia Gandhi is our daughter-in-law', was used. The party used positive slogans such as *'Mera Bharat meri shaan, yehi hai Congress ka armaan'*, meaning, 'My India is my pride, this is the Congress's desire'. The campaign also highlighted the late Rajiv Gandhi's acquittal from the Bofors scam.[25] It also used road shows, plying trucks with large pictures of Sonia and Rajiv Gandhi and TV sets playing videos.

The Congress did not use Rediffusion this time, but a small Delhi-based agency called Orchid, and Perfect Relations for its media management.

The 2004 election also saw Bollywood actors such as Dharmendra and Govinda being roped in for contesting as well as campaigning for major parties. Dharmendra fought on a BJP ticket from Bikaner, Rajasthan. His famous *Sholay* line, '*Gaon waalon, main aa gaya hoon*', and '*Mera gaon, mera desh*', became his campaign rhetoric. Wife Hema Malini also contested from the same party from Mathura, UP. The Congress fielded Govinda from Mumbai, whose catch line was, 'Let's put computers back on track.' Sunil Dutt, always a Congress loyalist, was once more fielded by the party.[26]

Sonia Gandhi won many admirers when she refused to take on the top job of the country but instead made Manmohan Singh the prime minister, retaining the Congress president's position for herself. This later led to two centres of power and the constant allegation from the Opposition and the media that Sonia Gandhi was running the government through remote control. But according to analysts, there was no change in the vote share of the Congress and the BJP between the 1999 and the 2004 elections, but the Congress managed to garner 31 extra seats because of the election dynamics, based on the system of the British electorate (also called the Westminster Electoral System), in which the principle of 'first past the post' is applied. Contrary to popular belief, more votes did not always assure victory, as what really mattered was how these votes were actually distributed across constituencies, which, in turn, could determine the winner of each constituency, each constituency remaining isolated from the rest.[27]

Reacting to the election outcome, *The Guardian* commented,

Under the slogan 'India Shining', the BJP had hoped that a bountiful monsoon, rising growth rates and a nascent peace process with Pakistan would have persuaded voters to give Mr Vajpayee another five years in office. However, Mrs Gandhi, who has grown into the role of political campaigner, tapped into concerns of the rural poor—at least 300 million people—who believed they were being left behind as the country's cities marched ahead.[28]

Reacting to the buzz around the India Shining campaign, *India Today* commented,

India Shining is often dubbed as one of the biggest reasons for the NDA government's failure to return to power at the Centre. Critics of the campaign, and there are aplenty, say the blitz crashed because of its 'lopsided' focus on urban growth story while neglecting the distress and backwardness of the rural landscape. Defenders of the campaign, however, continue to tout it as a good idea that was perhaps failed by the product (the NDA government).[29]

The fifteenth parliamentary election: 2009

The Congress did not manage a clear majority on its own in the fourteenth Lok Sabha election in 2004. Under the UPA, it completed its five-year term, from 2004 to 2009, by securing outside support from the Left parties—CPI(M), CPI, All India Forward Bloc and the Revolutionary Socialist Party—the SP and the BSP at different times during this tenure. In the fifteenth Lok Sabha election again, the Congress was short of majority on its own, but formed the government by securing 206 seats and a total of 262 seats with coalition partners. This, however, later got mired in myriad controversies.

The 2009 election campaign

For the 2009 campaign, the Congress bought the rights for the Oscar-winning soundtrack *Jai Ho* from the movie *Slumdog Millionaire*, which was used as the official campaign track by the party. 'Jai Ho' translates to 'Let there be victory', and the Congress hoped that the popular song would galvanize the masses during the almost month-long election season.

But the party got into trouble when the ECI sent it a notice for violating the model code of conduct, for naming the Commonwealth Games one of the achievements of the government in its ad campaign. The notice was served to the Ministry of Youth Affairs, the cabinet secretary and the chief secretary of Delhi.[30]

The BJP's catch phrase for the 2009 election campaign was '*Kushal Neta*', or 'Competent Leader'. It campaigned for strong laws such as the Prevention of Terrorism Act, or POTA, to combat insurgency. The 2009 election saw the use of technology by major players. Voice-overs and SMSs were used vigorously by the BJP. This was probably the first time that a contesting prime ministerial candidate, Vajpayee, used the voice-over technique to reach out to so many constituents with '*Namaskar, main Atal Bihari Vajpayee bol raha hoon*', or 'Hello, this is Atal Bihari Vajpayee speaking'.

Commenting on the outcome of the 2009 election, Zee News observed,

> Clearly, the main Opposition BJP's stunning drubbing proves that the BJP's campaign of 'strong leader and decisive government' and its deliberate branding of Dr Manmohan Singh as the 'weakest Prime Minister' failed to convince the electorate. In fact, Advani's personal tirade against the PM may have actually proved counterproductive. The unpredictably dismal performance of the BJP has sent the saffron brigade into soul-searching mode to determine the exact causes of its debacle and rethink whether they need to project a 'moderate BJP'.[31]

Years later, speaking at the Jaipur Chintan Shivir on 20 January 2013, the then prime minister Manmohan Singh expressed satisfaction for fulfilling most of the promises reflected in the party's manifestos in 2004 and 2009. The key point he made was that the Congress believed in inclusive growth and in that, it had succeeded a great deal through its various welfare schemes.

The Congress, during its second stint in 2009–2014, launched the Bharat Nirman campaign amid allegations of many scams and 'policy paralysis'.

Like the India Shining campaign, the government is believed to have used hundreds of crores of taxpayers' money to enlist its achievement. On the face of it, the campaign could score on all branding and positioning parameters. It talked about the party's achievements, especially in the rural sector. Using the testimonial route, the protagonists spoke about how their lives had changed in the times of the UPA, such as better roads, easy loans, special schemes for the youth, women, and scheduled castes and tribes, improved health facilities, the impact of education in making people aware of their rights, and rural employment through MGNREGA, among other things.

Both the India Shining and the Bharat Nirman campaigns were created by top-notch agencies, but helped neither the BJP in securing victory in 2004, nor the Congress in 2014.

Shifting from the Westminster democracy style of campaigning, Modi can be credited for bringing in the presidential style of personality-driven campaign with the slogan *'Ab ki baar Modi Sarkar'*, meaning, 'This time it will be the Modi government'.

The 2014 election is dubbed by many as the mother of all elections for various reasons—the style of campaigning, the huge amount of money involved and the active participation of the media in setting the agenda and clearly taking sides. This deserves a detailed analysis. Chapter 6 may be referred to for a multipronged perspective on the 2014 election campaign and the emergence of the star campaigner, Modi.

Discussion

A look at the various election campaigns over the past few decades gives one many insights into the campaigning style and strategies of various political parties. These are based on issues ranging from communalism to development, alleviation of poverty to corruption, and inflation to scams, leading the electorate to believe in a 'created' reality. Policy paralysis to the price of onions had incumbent governments losing their mandate. Americanization of elections, a term often used by analysts and critics, meant the use of big money, spin doctoring and a presidential style of campaigning revolving around personalities.

The Congress had a smooth sailing in politics until Nehru was alive. The party, from the beginning, had positioned itself as one for development and building a progressive India on two planks—'secular' and 'non-communal'. Later years saw the minority community drifting away from the Congress party and various leaders openly talking about being 'used'. The SP and the BSP have been the gainers from this drift, and did not shy away from using the plank in electoral campaigns. The assembly election in UP and elsewhere in 2017, however, changed the dynamics to an extent, as many Muslim-dominated areas returned to the Right-wing BJP candidates.

The emergence of Indira Gandhi, the internal squabbles within the Congress, the splintering of the party, followed by the emergence of the Congress (I) as the real party, the decimation of the Syndicate, and the sobriquets ranging from '*goongi gudia*' (dumb doll) to 'the only man in the cabinet' for Indira Gandhi, reflect in no uncertain terms the ups and downs, the struggles, the plots and the cunning employed by various players over a period of time for electoral gains.

The clincher was the one-liner used by Indira Gandhi, *'Woh kehte hein Indira hatao, mein kahti hoon garibi hatao.'* This caught the imagination of the electorate, which went on to become the highly saleable campaign tagline, *'Garibi Hatao'*, or 'Remove poverty'. It established Indira Gandhi as pro-poor and a leader who could be relied upon. The Bangladesh liberation only seemed to reinforce her stature. In the later part of the Sixties, her decision of bringing in the Green Revolution, the nationalization of banks and the withdrawal of privy purses of erstwhile kings consolidated her image as a decisive leader.

The proclamation of Emergency, the forcible sterilization of men as part of the family-planning drive, the gagging of the press and the losing of the 1977 election changed not only the politics but also some of the issues that would otherwise never have been touched with a bargepole. After the Congress (I)'s experiment with forced sterilization of men (Muslims came to believe that the measure was targeted against their community) and the electoral debacle that followed, the issue is considered politically incorrect, and all parties, including the Congress, have kept it away from their discourses both within and without the Parliament.

The Emergency and the following display of the power of public opinion in the 1977 election made the media realize its clout and, in a way, its responsibility as the watchdog of people's rights. The media became overtly defensive whenever there was an attempt to curb its freedom of speech. The media, especially the print media, was able to consolidate its position by becoming an active actor in the elections to follow. It will not be an exaggeration to say that the media has been setting the agenda through its editorials, opinionated articles, opinion polls, round-tables and prime-time discussions around all elections.

Top-notch advertising agencies and some of the most-well-known creative writers from the world of advertising were behind the election campaigns and communication strategies for top players 1984 onwards.

Of all the parties, only the Congress and the BJP have used mass media vigorously through paid campaigning, especially since 1984. One of the obvious reasons is that the donors from the corporate world have seen these two parties as the only viable alternatives at the centre, so both have been recipients of huge political donations. Regional parties, who are big players in their respective states, have also had no dearth of financial resources, as they have been kingmakers and have also participated in coalitions. In other words, big money power and the corporate nexus have been too obvious to be ignored.

The model code of conduct of the ECI has been more in the news for infringement by political parties rather than for their abidance.

Paid news during the past few elections has been one of the most-talked-about malpractices, but no concrete steps have yet been taken to combat it so far.

Despite the high-profile India Shining and Bharat Nirman campaigns by the BJP and the Congress as preludes to party campaigns, both the parties lost in 2004 and 2014 respectively, which makes one question the necessity of image-building ad campaigns involving thousands of crores of taxpayers' money.

Notes

1. http://www.smetimes.in/smetimes/general-elections-2009/miscellaneous/2009/Mar/23/history-of-lok-sabha-elections5584.html
2. Syndicate was the term used for the powerful lobby of leaders within the Congress party. In the early 1960s, it comprised K. Kamaraj, the former chief minister of Madras (now Chennai), Sanjiva Reddy, a leader from Andhra Pradesh who later became the president of India, S. Nijalingappa, former chief minister of Mysore (now Mysuru),

Atulaya Ghosh from West Bengal and S.K. Patil from Maharashtra. This group secretly debated on the issue of who the next prime minister should be after Nehru fell ill in 1963. The Syndicate managed control of the Congress working committee and had a say in who the next prime minister in Congress rule would be. Internal bickering and lack of trust among the members saw the Syndicate lose control of the committee. Indira Gandhi, in late 1969, split the party and it came to be known as the Congress (I).
https://revisitingindia.com/2013/07/01/the-syndicate-kingmakersof-india/

3. Operation Blue Star was conducted on 6 June 1984, in which the Army entered the sanctum sanctorum of the Sikh faith, Harmandir Sahib in Amritsar, leading to the killing of Jarnail Singh Bhindranwale, who was holed up there with his supporters and a huge arsenal of arms and ammunition.

4. "Video: When Rajiv Gandhi Justified the 1984 Killings", Swarajya, 20 November 2015
https://swarajyamag.com/lite/video-when-rajiv-gandhi-justified-the-1984-killings

5. Balakrishnan, Ajit, "Advance Trailers", Outlook, 19 October 2009
https://www.outlookindia.com/magazine/story/advance-trailers/262277

6. Gupta, Kanchan, "1984, This Week, When Congress Taught Tolerance to the World", *The Pioneer*, 1 November 2015

7. Khare, Harish, "The Modi Triumph: From 1984 to 2014 and Back to 1984", Scroll.in, 2 January 2015
http://scroll.in/article/697923/the-modi-triumph-from-1984-to-2014-and-back-to-1984

8. During the Janata Dal government, between 1977 and 1979, then prime minister Morarji Desai appointed a commission, with B.P. Mandal (a senior MP from Bihar) as chairman and five others as members, on 20 December 1978, to recommend reservations for the most backward class people. The commission submitted its report on 31 December

1980 to the then prime minister, Indira Gandhi. This report was not implemented by either Indira or Rajiv Gandhi for various political reasons, fearing backlash, but V.P. Singh brought it out of the closet for political dividends. Since then, there have been many agitations by various communities for reservation from time to time. The latest among these is the Jat agitation in Haryana in 2016, which saw property worth hundreds of crores destroyed, reports of huge loot and arson, and allegations of rape and molestation of women by hooligans.

9. https://www.eci.nic.in/archive/instruction/compendium/media_policy/mdpo84a.htm
10. Based on a personal interview of Bhaskar Rao by Jaishri Jethwaney on 18 December 1996
11. *The Indian Express*, 2 May 1991
12. *Business India*, 29 April–17 May 1991
13. S.P. Singh in a programme on election analysis on Doordarshan on 1 June 1991
14. Ibid
15. Jethwaney, Jaishri, "Tenth General Election—A Study", a research study conducted for the Indian Institute of Mass Communication, New Delhi, 1991
16. Ibid
17. Ibid
18. Ibid
19. Pai, Sudha, "Transformation of the Indian Party System: The 1996 Lok Sabha Elections", *Asian Survey*, University of California Press, Vol.36, No.12, pp.1177–1179
20. Vohra, Ranbir, *The Making of India: A Historical Survey*, M.E. Sharpe Inc, Armonk, New York, pp.288–290
21. "Elections 1996: 11th Lok Sabha Elections Saw Eclipse of the National Constituency Syndrome", *India Today*, 31 May 1996
http://indiatoday.intoday.in/story/elections-1996-11th-lok-sabha-elections-saw-eclipse-of-the-national-constituency-syndrome/1/280693.html

22. http://cpim.org/documents/1999-LS-Election_Review.pdf
23. "The Untold Story of How BJP Lost 2004 Elections", Guruprasad's Portal http://guruprasad.net/posts/the-untold-story-of-how-bjp-lost-2004-elections/
24. "The Great Indian Election Slogan Warfare", Guruprasad's Portal (http://guruprasad.net/posts/the-great-indian-election-slogan-warfare/), and "21 Election Slogans That Decided the Fate of Indian Politics", Scoopwhoop.com (https://www.scoopwhoop.com/Election-Slogans-Indian-Politics/#.5oa7nw9py)
25. "Managing Elections, Congress Style", Rediff.com, 18 March 2004 http://www.rediff.com/election/2004/mar/18espec.htm
26. "Elections 2004: Bollywood Stars, Celebrities Hit Campaign Trail", *India Today*, 19 April 2004 http://indiatoday.intoday.in/story/bollywood-stars-turningpoliticians-campaign-for-congress-bjp-april2004/1/196215.html
27. https://www.quora.com/Why-did-the-Congress-win-in-2004-General-Elections-inspite-of-good-governance-by-the-Vajpayee-Government
28. Ramesh, Randeep, "Shock Defeat for India's Hindu Nationalists", *The Guardian*, 14 May 2004 https://www.theguardian.com/world/2004/may/14/india.randeepramesh
29. Bagga, Bhuvan, "What Makes NDA's 'India Shining' Campaign the 'Worst' Poll Strategy in Indian History", *India Today*, 14 May 2013 http://indiatoday.intoday.in/story/nda-india-shining-worst-poll-strategy/1/270916.html
30. www.hindu.com. Archived from the original on 28 July 2009. Retrieved 6 February 2014
31. Srivastava, Ritesh K., "Election 2009 Dissected: How Parties Cut the Vote Pie", Zee News, 30 August 2011 http://zeenews.india.com/home/election-2009-dissected-how-parties-cut-the-vote-pie_532875.html

6

THE SIXTEENTH PARLIAMENTARY ELECTIONS: THE MOTHER OF ALL ELECTIONS; THE EMERGENCE OF MODI THE CAMPAIGNER

> 'It is absurd to hold that a man should be ashamed of an inability to defend himself with his limbs but not ashamed of an inability to defend himself with speech and reason, for the use of rational speech is more distinctive of a human being than the use of his limbs.'
>
> —ARISTOTLE

In a human being, there are always characteristics inherent to his/her personality, but a lot can be acquired. In times when politics is more akin to a market activity and politicians to brands, it is not uncommon to see brand managers and savvy advertising specialists employed to help politicians find favour with voters. *'Jancha, parkha, khara'*, the BJP's tagline for Vajpayee during the 1999 election, to *'Sonia nahin yeh aandhi hai, yeh toh doosri Indira Gandhi hai'* by the Congress in the 2004 election are just two cases in point. Brand management experts feel that the value provided at a point of time is not perennial; considerable effort is required to not only retain the value constantly but also upgrade it to match the voter's expectations and the strategies of the rivals. Modi's emergence on the national electoral scene in 2013–14 changed the whole grammar of campaigning.

In this age of information, the media has become an indispensable tool, especially in election campaigning. With thousands of hours of cumulative programming available on various channels and a host of 24-hour news channels, the scope is immense for politicians during campaigning. The talk shows, discussions and panel meetings are doing what paid advertising could never achieve.

Brand experts, while positioning politicians and parties, often use a brand identity prism. Let us look at how it works:

Jean-Noël Kapferer's Brand Identity Prism

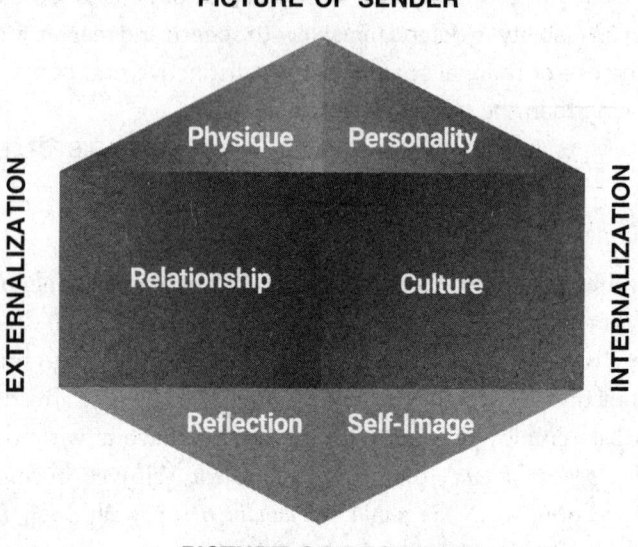

According to Kapferer, brand identity is represented diagrammatically by a hexagonal prism with six characteristics.

- Physique. A combination of independent characteristics, a kind of lifestyle association.
- Personality. A brand has a personality, it may also acquire a character, say, of being arrogant, modest or kind. How it acquires it depends on how it has been positioned and the experience the consumer has had with the brand.
- Culture. This facet relates to the basic principles governing the brand in its outward signs, for example, products and communications. The product is the physical embodiment and vector of this culture.
- Relationship. A brand according to this typology is a relationship, an opportunity for an intangible exchange between persons.
- Reflection. A brand reflects a consumer's image. Reflection is not necessarily the target but the image of that target, which the brand offers to the public; it's a type of identification.
- Self-image. If reflection is the target's outward mirror, the self-image is the target's internal mirror, which may be either prominent or dormant; through our attitude towards certain brands, we develop a certain inner relationship with ourselves.

These six facets define brand identity and its potential territory. The brand identity prism demonstrates that these facets form a structured whole. However, each facet is dependent on the others. A brand exists only if it communicates. The communication allows the receiver to imagine the image of the sender. The receiver is the person who is at the receiving end. So, obviously, there is both a sender and a receiver in the process. Hence, in the identity prism, according to Kapferer, the facets to the left—physique, relationship and reflection—are the social facets, which give the brand its outward expression. All three are tangible factors. The facets to the right—personality, culture and self-image—are incorporated within the brand. These are the intangibles, but just as important as the tangible ones to make a brand complete.

If we were to deconstruct Modi in 2013–14 as the prime ministerial candidate based on Kapferer's brand identity model, on the social front, we would have the characteristic of physique—he was projected as disciplined, emotional (he would break down on screen at times) and a kind ascetic, reinforced by the narrative created around him as 'Bal Narendra', someone who was not really interested in worldly comforts, and was almost on the verge of taking sanyas. But at same time, he carried the huge baggage of the Gujarat riots of 2002, reinforced time and again by the media and the Opposition, and the description used for him by Sonia Gandhi, then Congress president—'*maut ka saudagar*'.

On the cultural front, related to the governing of the brand, through product and communication, he had on offer the 'Gujarat model' of governance, which many may not have understood but nonetheless went along with, given the 'policy paralysis' scenario created by the media discourse against the incumbent UPA government.

The facets to the right—personality, culture and self-image—the intangibles, helped in creating a complete Brand Modi. He was seen as someone coming from a meagre background, who went to school but helped his father, a tea-seller, a Sangh pracharak, an educated youngster and someone who gave up family for a larger cause. Leaving a young wife was not seen within the brand as an act of inhumanity but one done in the interest of a larger cause, amplified by the discourse on how Lord Buddha left his wife and young son (the name of the wife incidentally was the same for both, Yashoda) for higher goals for humanity.

As Modi's image grew larger and more powerful from one rally to another, from one discourse to another, using all kinds of rhetoric—deliberative and forensic—it was not only him who believed he could deliver, but even sceptics within the party who grew to believe he could. Modi, thus, came out as an aspirational brand across the voter spectrum.

In retrospect, just before the 1999 election, the Indian Institute of Mass Communication undertook an interesting study to assess popular leaders on the parameters of the brand identity prism to find out how the youth perceived those they were likely to vote for. The leaders in the study were Vajpayee, Sonia Gandhi, Sushma Sawaraj, Jyoti Basu, Mayawati, Chandra Babu Naidu, J. Jayalalithaa and Mamata Banerjee, among others. The sample had 585 first- and second-time voters comprising young college students, both male and female. Out of the 585 respondents, 185 were second- or third-time voters and 348 were either first-time voters or those who did not vote in the 1998 elections. As many as 438 were in the age group of 18–24, and 89 voters were over 24 years. The study was conducted in Delhi, but as it covered all the country's premier universities and institutes, it had a fair representation of the demography.[1]

Just to provide one or two instances from the study, based on the brand identity model, Vajpayee, who went on to become the prime minister in 1999, got a high score on experience, uprightness, honesty and liberal views, despite his being from a party perceived as one with an orthodox Hindutva agenda. Hence, the desired response of those who were likely to vote for him was reflected as: 'I am a liberal, so I will vote for him.' This section of respondents was expected to believe in the philosophy that Vajpayee represented—traditional but flexible, in other words, pragmatic.

The respondents were asked to tick any two attributes among the many listed below, which, in their view, best defined the politician: visionary, shrewd, experienced, mass appeal, honest/upright, aggressive, abrasive, incoherent, analytical, charismatic, dishonest, scheming, uninspiring, uncharismatic, survivor, inexperienced, elegant.

Sonia Gandhi was voted the highest for her inexperience. Over

59 per cent respondents perceived 'inexperience' as her strongest attribute. Similarly, over 35 per cent respondents considered her a poor communicator. However, she came out a winner as far as her dress sense was concerned. As many as 65 per cent respondents felt that she looked elegant. Shrewdness, dishonesty and a scheming nature were not considered strong attributes of her personality, as perceived by the youth. About 17 per cent respondents also saw her as charismatic.[2]

The study provided a few interesting insights into the voters' thought process, including what they had on their latent mind, and their self-articulated input on various politicians based on their acquired information and knowledge coming from various sources, including the media, which often impacted voting behaviour.

Modi the brand

The 2014 parliamentary election in the context of PM Modi is often referred to by brand experts as a photo-finish study in brand-building. His election campaign in the 2014 Lok Sabha polls, many believe, is a classic example of how to prepare and successfully implement a marketing and branding campaign. Modi was all-pervasive on the media, being the prime-time news subject for months. Irrespective of one's faith, ideology and voting decision, there was no escaping him. However, this was not the first time that a prime ministerial candidate in India had been exposed to brand-building.

One thing different about the 2014 election strategy on the part of Modi was that the campaign, with its decisive slogan *'Ab ki baar, Modi Sarkar'*, was not talking about BJP per se but about Modi, making the campaign revolve around a single personality.

Modi's public outreach programme and strategy, coupled with his gift of the gab in communicating key messages, overshadowed all other brands, even from his own party. Not only political strategists but even academics and brand experts sat in awe of how an almost perfect Brand Modi emerged, despite the baggage he carried post Godhra riots in Gujarat. Commenting on the national euphoria created by Modi's campaign, in contrast to that of his challenger Arvind Kejriwal's, *The Economic Times* team trailing the campaign commented, 'As BJP commanders such as Arun Jaitley, Amit Shah and Nalin Kohli sit in the air-conditioned comfort of five-star hotels with embedded journalists, strategizing and munching snacks and organizing lavish pressers, Kejriwal drives on pitted and unpaved roads without the fetters of overpowering security into depths of darkness that is an Indian village.'[3]

Making of Brand Modi

Let's look at the branding of Modi, which some feel was born out of compulsion. Prior to Modi's emergence, the BJP had been branded as communal and intolerant by the Opposition. The party needed to redefine itself in the competitive Indian political scene, so under the circumstances, the pitch of good governance and development suited it the most. From the market research perspective, the party should be credited as the first to recognize and adapt to the fundamental shift in the composition of voters and their concomitant aspirations. It presented an existing product in new packaging, and hence seized the opportunity to project a new face to address the target audience, i.e., the average voter's aspirations. This led to the birth of Brand Modi.

A person who only had a few takers as a prime ministerial candidate in October 2013, including in his own party, was suddenly catapulted as the only choice in a matter of months. Only ascribing it to a smart campaign would be unfair; his inherent resilience and inner strength—a 'do or die' attitude, an *'abhi nahin toh kabhi nahin'* attitude—had an equal, if not larger role to play.

Modi the product: The image of a man with humble origins, an ascetic kind of background, free of corruption, diligent and leading a disciplined life made Modi that perfect mascot of the BJP who could challenge the Opposition. The branding of Modi and the presidential-style campaigning were two apt attempts to redefine Indian politics—a space where everyone was competing. The branding of Modi was a well-crafted strategy by the Rashtriya Swayamsevak Sangh (RSS) and the BJP. However, ironically, what became the BJP's biggest advantage was the prime ministerial candidate from the Congress pitted against Modi—then a reluctant and inexperienced Rahul Gandhi, who still had a long way to go to reach the stature and cunning of a professional politician.

The promise of Brand Modi: Good governance and economic development through the Gujarat model were presented on a platter to voters. Not many understood what it was, but the average voter deconstructed it as the viable alternative to the corruption- and scam-riddled incumbent UPA government. At the same time, this strategy was also aimed at allaying the fears of voters who were uncomfortable with Modi's past—the allegations of his complicity in the 2002 Godhra riots. Modi's endeavour was to create a narrative around secularism versus pseudo-secularism. The entire brand promise was posited on the aspiration of good governance, i.e., 'minimum government, maximum governance', which was supposed to change Indian politics forever and make the BJP the natural choice to form the government.

Modi's ability to become larger than the party that nurtured him lay in his ability to listen to the nation's murmurs and whispers, and being able to take advantage of the simmering anger, hopelessness and helplessness of the common man. This is the basic rule of marketing—listen to your customers and empathize with them. His traits of being organized, proactive, confident and in command of things subtly connected with the 'created' persona of the ruler archetype, which is not uncommon in the world of marketing. In such cases, not only does the brand become bigger than its creator, but it also has the capability to revitalize and rejuvenate itself. Some cases in point are Maggi becoming bigger than Nestlé, and Lifebuoy becoming bigger than Unilever in terms of recall and resonance. To cite yet another example, what iMac and iPod did to Apple Inc. is what Narendra Modi did to the BJP.

Prior to Modi, the BJP brand, according to analysts, was on the brink of irrelevance vis-à-vis what it stood for. Its Hindutva identity resonated deeply with the Partition generation, but its effect had weakened for successive generations. Demographically, India is one of the youngest nations in the world, and as of the 2011 census, with more than 65 per cent of the population below 35 years—this did not seem to be working for the party.

Catching up with the youth, on 6 February 2013, more than six months before he was named the BJP's prime ministerial choice, Modi addressed students at Delhi's prestigious Shri Ram College of Commerce (SRCC), where he talked about Gujarat's model of development. One gets an interesting insight from this too. Instead of Delhi's two iconic colleges—Hindu and St. Stephen's—he chose SRCC because of its student profiling. Those studying commerce would understand his economic model more than the others. He spoke passionately about the need for speed in government decision-making, and the need to improve the skills of the youth to accelerate economic growth. That speech won him many young admirers that day.

Modi's efforts to connect with the youth and urban voters were also given a boost by his pro-business persona. Business leaders, such as Ratan Tata and billionaire brothers Mukesh and Anil Ambani, all came out in open praise of Modi and his administration in Gujarat. This allowed Modi to build his brand as a progressive leader who had the ability to deliver economic results—the single-biggest leitmotif of this campaign that has allowed it to cut through caste bias, among other things.

Modi created an identity that resonated with far more people and far deeper than the BJP did. The Gujarat model threw in words such as governance, roads, electricity, women's safety, peace, industry and education, supported by statistics. Modi's storytelling style and his narrative at rallies would often touch an emotional chord with the audience and provide a compelling visual imagery. Once, when talking about women's safety, he related the Gujarat scenario, in which young girls, often with a lot of ornaments on their person, could safely and without fear, and return home alone at night after attending the Navratra festival. For the emotional consumer, he tapped into the despair and hopelessness that seemed to have gripped the people of the country then, and projected the image of both the outlaw and the ruler. He was perceived as an icon of disruption and rebellion against the corrupt way of things then. It was this countercultural streak that appealed to the youth, who desired change the most. In contrast, the average youngster did not relate to Rahul Gandhi, despite him being much younger than Modi. The reason was obvious—he neither had the strong persona of Modi, nor did he have anything substantive to offer.

With his gift of the gab, Modi the orator delivered scores of speeches in his untiring and overzealous campaigning from one state to another. He highlighted issues such as the slowing economic growth, high inflation and lack of new jobs—issues that immediately resonated with the young and urban voters—while blaming the Congress-led UPA government for its inability to solve these national problems. The media added to the created narrative of 'policy paralysis' against the incumbent UPA government.

As soon as the election was announced, Modi's marketing team unleashed print, television and radio advertisements with the same themes he had been addressing in his rallies and road shows. The advertisements, some in Modi's own recorded voice, reached out to people asking for their votes. It also tapped into social media platforms such as Facebook, YouTube and Twitter to magnify the impact of the advertising and branding campaigns.

The impact of this relentless campaigning was felt across age groups, geographies and sections of society. NaMo, the sobriquet used for Narendra Modi, imbued his name with a reverence very specific to the Indian context. The Sanskrit expression '*Namo-namah*' evokes images of bowing in reverence before the supreme entity being addressed. In contrast, Rahul Gandhi was given the nickname RaGa, which he did not make effective use of.

However, against the sobriquet 'Pappu' for Rahul Gandhi, Modi got an unflattering nickname of his own, 'Fenku', from Congress supporters. However, in analysis, the term 'Pappu', used to refer to someone childish, did more harm to Rahul than 'Fenku' did to Modi. 'Fenku', means someone who exaggerates, which sounded less harmful than 'Pappu' for a leader. To analyse it further, in the context of 'Fenku', the deconstruction can be that only someone who understands things can exaggerate, but for someone who cannot decipher anything (Pappu), what can be expected of him?

No marketing or advertising campaign can sell a substandard product. The product must have an aspirational value or fulfil the promises it makes, which, unfortunately, at that time, the Congress candidate did not have. The Congress did not lack in spending power or in getting some great marketing genius to create a befitting campaign. But, somehow, the party seemed to have given up even before a fight. There was reticence on its part to name the prime ministerial candidate. Whenever cornered by the media, the spokespersons would evade the question or, at best, say that the leader was always selected after the election as per the party's tradition.

The biggest push for Modi, according to analysts, came from the overt support and advocacy of corporate leaders.

The three Ps of political marketing—posters, propoganda and persuasion

The primary aim of political warfare is to win votes, by building preference and shaping perception. The challenge of preference-building is that it has to be accomplished in a short period. This was not a classic marketing warfare, but marshalling the four Ps of marketing—product, price, promotion and place. Marketing in politics is more about the four Cs: cause, constituency, comparative advertising and celebrity endorsements.

Cause is the starting point: What does the party stand for? Why does the party exist? What does the prime ministerial candidate stand for? There can be many causes on offer—development, safety, jobs, prices, pride, honesty, secularism and governance.

The election saw multiple voter segments. The voters were young, idealistic and sought a motivating argument to come and vote. The best argument for this group was economic—the promise of jobs and a brighter future. For urban voters, impacted by inflation, safety and loss of jobs, the cause was good, with the promise of clean governance and accountable politics. The rural poor, in the Indian context, have always been the largest chunk in the vote bank. The best causes of the past have revolved around the poor—the best being '*Garibi Hatao*'. For the rural poor, the cause is often socioeconomic and includes the ability of the government to support them via subsidized food rates, etc.

In marketing, this is labelled as consumer promotions. In politics, the voter knows that a freebie or a promotion is permanent and rarely withdrawn, irrespective of who comes to power. So just a sop will not work as a cause—it has to be packaged with another cause. Legacy works in times of good governance and economic results; it was not expected that legacy would be flaunted by any party in the run-up to the 2014 election. The context of 2014 was different. India Shining as a campaign was flaunted because the then government thought it would pay a dividend. Similarly, MGNREGA was flaunted as a governance model in 2009, which won them that year's election. But 2014 was the time when there was no such legacy to talk about.

Constituency is the equivalent of local markets in marketing. It was crucial for parties to think differently of the 543 Lok Sabha constituencies. The candidate who presented the best chance in the constituency was expected to both optimize many variables and be able to microtarget. The party was also expected to manage spurned candidates who played spoiler in at least a fifth of the constituencies. 'Think national but choose local' was the best strategy, similar to brand marketing campaigns. The NDA partners were expected to micromanage the choice of saleable candidates where they had a stronghold.

Comparative advertising, as they say, is the cornerstone of political marketing. The idea was to portray competitors in an unfavourable manner without being perceived as attacking them. Political advertising parameters helped in creating the phenomenon of FUD—fear, uncertainty and doubt. Many empirical studies have shown that comparative advertising lowers the image of the attacked candidate without affecting the attacking candidate, because voters believe negative advertising gives them more information to make a better decision. Comparative advertising works on a game plan that includes facts that can be represented, revisiting past comments of candidates, voting records of candidates, past friendships, etc. In India, private lives have so far been out of the comparative script, but in this election, anonymous digital identities played this card too, but not to the extent one sees in the US. The Trump-Hillary campaign of 2016 hit one of the lowest levels in history.[4]

Then come **celebrity endorsements**. The initial celebrity quotient was glamour. With rapid media growth in the past decade, we have seen celebrity commentators such as editors, TV anchors, former diplomats and government servants all offering their endorsements for the benefit of the voter. Parties roped in influential social commentators and fed them with talking points to build preference, especially among undecided voters.

Political parties unleashed their teams on TV, print and social media. Right to Information (RTI) was used as a reference check for celebrity commentary. First-time voters, social media targeting and speedy response to unfolding events were expected to decide the outcome of the election—and it did. All three were interlinked. In the 725-million-strong electorate, 150 million were first-time voters, and more than half of them were on social media. This group was targeted, and it responded digitally in equal measure, as they wanted their voice to matter. It was the first election campaign in India that made such vigorous use of social media and information technology. The social media team of Modi responded in real time to voters and potential voters.

Modi's team

Modi's positioning from a regional, Right-wing politician to a decisive leader with a clear national development agenda—the one best suited to take India forward—is nothing short of extraordinary from the perspective of strategy. Senior BJP leaders, including Piyush Goyal and Ajay Singh, handled the overall media strategy, backed by a task force constituted to handle Modi's campaign in Varanasi. Prashant Kishor, who was the campaign manager for Modi's professional support team via the Citizens for Accountable Governance (CAG), executed initiatives such as Chai Pe Charcha, 3D rallies, constituency-level analytics and a powerful digital media campaign. Advertising legends such as Ogilvy & Mather's Piyush Pandey, McCann Worldgroup's Prasoon Joshi and Madison World's Sam Balsara lent the campaign their skills at various levels.

Advertising agency Soho Square, part of the WPP Group, handled television, radio and print campaigns with catchy slogans such as 'Ab ki baar Modi Sarkar'.

The Modi archetype was a towering, strong, all-knowing and unwavering personality. To create the father figure, Modi's team invoked tales from children's books and comics. Invariably and understandably, those were the tales of heroism involving a precocious Bal Narendra. What else would you call the story of a child swimming across a crocodile-infested lake to plant the Indian flag on a memorial? The child, when he came of age, walked away from his family to devote himself to a public cause. Modi's team faced three main challenges when it set out to project him as the country's next prime minister.

- The three-time Gujarat chief minister was a regional brand trying to go national.
- He was a 63-year-old politician seeking to connect with the youth, and this was no easy task, considering that the sixteenth parliamentary election had almost 150 million first-time voters. Modi, who rarely chose to speak in English, was also trying to connect with the urban middle-class audience, which was becoming more politically conscious.
- Most importantly, Modi still carried the taint of the 2002 anti-Muslim riots in Gujarat.

It is not easy for a brand to go from regional to national, and so it was with Modi too. The dilution of the only other national brand, the Congress, and the common underlying need for change, however, helped. If a brand could tap into a common underlying need and connect it to benefits it can offer, it could go national. From the marketing world, one can take the example of Haldiram's and Saravana Bhavan, both of which managed the feat famously. They targeted the overall underlying need for tasty north Indian snacks and south Indian food, and took their brands national.

But there is a difference between a regional brand going national and a regional politician going national. Modi was known outside Gujarat even before he decided to move beyond the state, just as it was with Nitish Kumar, chief minister of Bihar, and J. Jayalalithaa, former chief minister of Tamil Nadu. But these regional leaders didn't venture out of their home states during the elections. Modi did. And he did it on a massive scale—he attended more than 5,000 events and 470 political rallies across the length and breadth of the country.

Testing the brand before the elections

The one event that, perhaps, helped Modi the most in making a mark on the national scene was the shifting of the Tata Motors factory in 2008 for the Nano minicar from West Bengal to Gujarat. Farmers in West Bengal, backed by the firebrand politician Mamata Banerjee, now the state's chief minister, had been protesting land acquisition for the plant by Tata Motors. Modi provided the automobile company land and other incentives almost overnight. In a televised interview, he compared Gujarat to Yashoda, who mothered Krishna when he was brought to her as an infant after escaping the tyranny of his uncle Kans. In the process, Modi established himself as a champion of industry and development.

Challenge: shaking off the stigma

The biggest challenge Brand Modi faced was diverting public attention away from the 2002 communal riots in Gujarat, which claimed the lives of more than 1,000 people, mostly Muslims. Initially, Modi's supporters in the BJP attempted to engage in public debate and highlight the clean chit given by the courts to wash off the stigma. Then they changed tack. They toned down the Hindutva rhetoric and focused on Modi's more recent past and his development record in Gujarat. Modi knew that all else aside, people aspired for a better life. He still offered Hindutva, but with the right dilution.

Marketing gurus cite the examples of Cadbury, PepsiCo and Coca-Cola, which battled problems related to brand taint. Cadbury fought its way out of a controversy related to worms in its chocolates, while the two beverage giants faced allegations of pesticides in their colas. The best way for a tainted brand to overcome a challenge is to not talk too much about it, acknowledge it happened and move on. The more one talks about the taint, the more the memory of that event is activated in the target market, and the more the consumer remembers it. The BJP and Modi did not talk about the Gujarat riots. And if they did, they kept it to a minimum. Modi never apologized for it. According to Y.L.R Moorthi, a professor of Marketing at the Indian Institute of Management, Bengaluru, 'He did give an account of reflections on the event [the riots]. He seemed to say that he was pained about the event, but didn't say sorry.' It did not matter if Modi was wrong; he never publicly admitted to any wrongdoing. But, at the same time, without ever saying so, he took corrective measures to navigate out of it.[5]

The ideal model

Not so long ago, the words that were used to describe Modi included authoritarian, megalomaniac and communal. But the creators of Brand Modi focused on building Modi's image as self-made, strong, efficient, inspiring and incorruptible. They dealt with the taint by not dealing with it. Instead, the image Modi projected was of a sincere, credible and committed leader. He convinced people that he could improve their lot. This is the leitmotif the marketing arsenal of the BJP worked to amplify. No media can help create that kind of consistency.

The onion peel model for Modi during the 2014 election

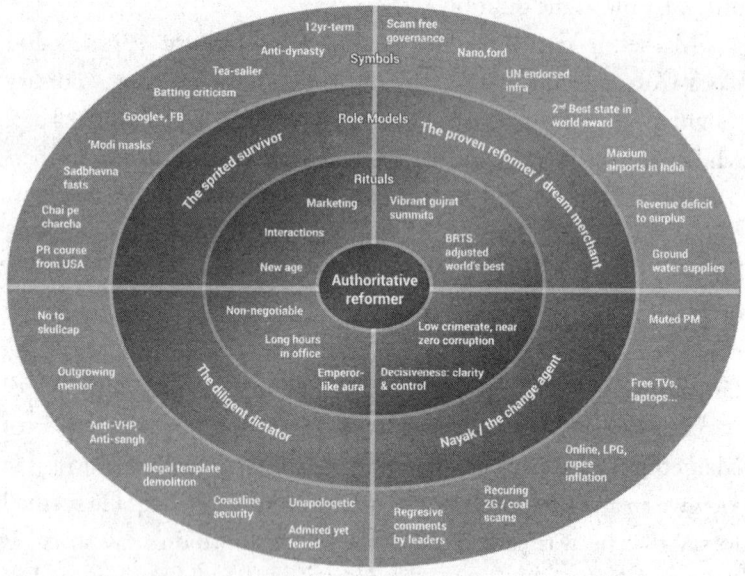

Theory behind the onion peel model

Academics and researchers have often explored the manifest and latent importance of brand meaning. The premise is that the brands that people find different in a good way are the ones they are willing to pay a premium price for. There are some very distinct layers of how a brand is perceived, and marketers need to work differently to motivate the people on each level.

There are three main layers of brand meaning, starting from the outside of the 'onion' to the layers within. Each layer can influence the layers below it or be influenced itself.

Cultural meaning: This is the broad context in which consumers come to appreciate what a brand stands for and respond to it accordingly. An example would be a brand such as Tata Salt in India, which, in the past, has sought to leverage Indian pride in its ad campaigns. Brands also seek to leverage popular culture by teaming up with celebrities. And some brands are so strong that they are not just influenced by popular culture but also play a part in influencing it. Brands such as Google and Facebook have shaped the world in which we now live and have, as a result, earned a unique status in the minds of many.

Community meaning: This may seem like a more granular version of the cultural meaning. Community does not just denote a local community, it refers to any group of associated people: colleagues, and people who support the same club or pursue the same hobbies and interests. Other people might refer to these groups as tribes, but that implies a strong degree of allegiance and, as it is common knowledge that people can easily be influenced by those around them, these different communities have the power to expose us to new brands and influence our perceptions of them. Once again, a few strong brands have the power to attract a community around the brand itself, such as Harley-Davidson and Apple.

Individual meaning: Individual meaning is probably far more motivating than the collective meaning. This is the domain where small differences can have big consequences. A brand just needs to be different enough for someone to choose it and pay a premium for it. The source of that meaningful difference may be so unique or trivial that it may not be readily appreciated, even by the person buying the brand.

The idea behind the onion peel model in large measure is influenced by the product-level wagon wheel, proposed by Philip Kotler in his book *Marketing Management*. He talked about three layers of products or services—namely, core, actual and augmented. The onion peel thus takes a cue from that wheel and expands it to individual, community and cultural, or to the core-value preposition, actual-value preposition and augmented-value preposition of a brand.

Modi's onion peel explained

At the core of the onion peel is the authoritative reformer. This is the core brand image of the person and his USP—his personality trait.

Peeling to the next layer, or what is called the actual level, as per the wagon wheel, he is:

- A proven reformer or a dream merchant
- 'Nayak': the change agent
- The diligent dictator
- The spirited survivor

The 'rituals' performed to explain this next peel are:

- His marketing acumen—the way he created and marketed a flagship event, Vibrant Gujarat
- The Metro and Bus Rapid Transit System (BRTS), which was set up for Vibrant Gujarat, is adjudged one of the best in the world
- His emperor-like aura, non-negotiable attitude, long hours in office, low crime rate, near-zero corruption, decisiveness, clarity and control

The symbols that are projected to show this image of him are: His immaculate record of twelve years, the tea-seller image, the Modi masks and the famous Chai Pe Charcha are some of the symbols that helped create this aura around Brand Modi.

Media matters

The sixteenth parliamentary election was keenly followed by many the world over, including the media. The interest increased manifold the moment the BJP announced its prime ministerial candidate, Narendra Damodar Modi. *The New York Times* reported, 'India may be the world's most populous democracy, but election campaigns here are often fueled by hate and soaked in blood. By choosing Mr Modi, a fiery orator who once peppered his speeches with anti-Muslim slurs, the Bharatiya Janata Party has raised the prospect that this election could be the deadliest in decades.'[6]

In the same article, Gardiner Harris says, 'Mr Modi, 63, refused requests over months for an interview (he rarely speaks to Western news organizations)'.[7]

There was a general perception among Indian journalists too that Modi was avoiding the media. One did not see him addressing any press conference or reaching out to any television studio. In the meantime, Times Now news anchor Arnab Goswami was able to get a long one-on-one interview with Rahul Gandhi. What could have established him as the leader of his party or a Modi challenger did just the reverse. He emerged as a person who was unsure of everything, political or otherwise. His facts were not in place, he seemed confused and in his own world, rattling out answers to whatever questions were posed. The contrast between Modi and him became too obvious to be ignored.

Modi, on his part, did not have a very friendly press on his campaign trail. In fact, in one of the rallies, he referred to journalists as 'news traders', earning the ire of a well-known journalist, who openly said that if Modi was elected, life would not be easy for the likes of him.

Then one Saturday night, viewers found Modi on *Aap Ki Adalat*, an hour-long programme on India TV anchored by Modi's friend and well-wisher Rajat Sharma before an invited audience, most of whom seemed to be in awe of the person. Modi was established as a determined leader who was out to change lives. After becoming PM, Modi was invited by Rajat Sharma to celebrate two decades of his show. Modi, on the live programme, acknowledged the platform this programme had given him to reach out to Indians around election time.

Modi as PM has kept up the same attitude—there have been no media meets in the last three years. He does not take the media with him on his many trips abroad. Some ascribe this to his bad experience with journalists during the 2002 Gujarat riots. Sardesai, among many others, had openly spoken of the difficult times ahead for some of them if Modi became prime minister. With more than 43.2 million followers on social networking sites, Modi is more interactive there than on mainstream media such as the press and the television. This consistent keeping of the media at bay has reinforced Brand Modi's stand vis-à-vis the media and journalists. This, despite the fact that some well-known journalists with Rightist views had appeared on various news channels during Modi's campaign, defending him and the party's stand on myriad issues.

Now that Modi has formed the government—and is, in fact, on the cusp of another election in 2019—a hypothetical question remains: If Modi had given a free hand to the media, what could possibly have been the outcome?

The campaign that changed India's political landscape

The overwhelming response to Modi's campaign for good governance and development resulted in a landslide victory for the BJP in the sixteenth parliamentary election. Through the hundreds of rallies Modi addressed, he remained focused, talking mostly of development, despite his critics from the Congress and other 'secular' parties repeatedly mentioning the Godhra riots in their discourse.

Modi, time and again, emphasized the Gujarat model, of providing 24x7 electricity and water to all villages in Gujarat. Commenting on the Gujarat model of development, *The Economist* wrote, 'Gujarat is richer, enjoys faster GDP growth and a greater intensity of jobs and industry than India as a whole. Mr Modi's reputation for clean government and economic competence rests on his record here. When Indians voted for him in great numbers last May, it was in large part because they wanted the country run as Gujarat is. His impact on the state is nevertheless contested.'[8]

While Modi sarcastically referred to Rahul Gandhi as 'shehzada', or prince, Congress leaders derided him with epithets such as 'Hitler' and 'fascist'. As mentioned earlier, Sonia Gandhi had also referred to Modi as '*maut ka saudagar*' and said he indulged in '*khoon ki kheti*', or the harvest of blood and gore, during the 2007 assembly election.

The problem with the Congress campaign as election time approached was that it did not take advantage of the various achievements of the government, especially in regard to the dozens of welfare schemes, such as rural employment, the health mission, food security, etc. Its surrogate Bharat Nirman campaign, which used thousands of crores of public money, met the same fate as the NDA's India Shining campaign.

Keen observers of India's political scene have noticed that the expectation of the people over the past few decades has risen, thanks to exposure to education, the mass media—especially television—greater connectivity through mobile phones, and migration to other states, resulting in the emergence of an aspirational middle class. They are no longer happy with just freebies. They look for jobs and aspire for better lives. P. Chidambaram, the finance minister in UPA II, acknowledged as much when he said, 'India has moved from a petitioner society to an aspirational one. Treating people as petitioners is a mistake... Even the poor demand a better life and are no longer resigned to their fate.'[9]

It was surprising that the groundswell of support Modi received from almost across India went unrecognized not only by his detractors but also by party stalwarts such as L.K. Advani and Murali Manohar Joshi. In fact, Advani, after Modi's victory, called him a great 'event manager'. To quote him, 'I will not call Narendrabhai my protégé, but I have never seen a more brilliant and efficient events manager.'[10]

Some have pointed out that the BJP and Modi have spent a large amount of money on television and newspaper advertisements, in addition to Modi's whirlwind tours all over the country, which won him his victory.

Case study: the 2014 BJP campaign

Modi's campaign was about creating experience and engagement for the audience. There was a reason behind all communication, and Modi's team of communication and marketing experts worked relentlessly to reach out to all corners of India.

Let's look at some of the characteristics of the campaign that saw the unprecedented rise of Brand Modi.

Launch: PR to build credibility

Modi started his campaign way before the election. The campaign did not take off with heavy mass media budgets but chose a soft and surrogate route. Modi's first objective was to build relevance around the chosen positioning. He, therefore, spoke of his work in Gujarat to increase awareness and build his image as the agent of development and change. He promoted Gujarat as a tourist destination and rolled out a well-designed and professional campaign with Amitabh Bachchan as the state's brand ambassador.

The media later reported that this gave Gujarat immediate recall value as a tourist destination for many travellers.

Modi's initial communication strategy focused on winning international acclaim through appearances and mentions in *Time*, *The Economist*, *The New York Times*, *The Wall Street Journal* and other leading US publications. This forced the national media to focus on him. Modi and his team understood the Indian colonial mindset, in which it is seen that we tend to acknowledge and reward those the outside world does.

Modi started his campaign in February 2013 and accepted invitations to events that catered to key demographics across the country. These included institutions such as the SRCC in New Delhi, the FICCI Ladies Organisation, Google's Big Tent, the India Today Conclave, and Fergusson College in Pune, where he first articulated his 'Gujarat model' in detail. His aim was to create bottom-up pressure on the BJP leadership. Modi was careful about choosing interview opportunities. His appearance on chat shows was timed appropriately. He also happened to be the first Indian politician to make effective use of the social media and digital space.

> ***Key communication lesson***: *It is not about PR or advertising, or a loud or soft launch, but knowing when and what to say.*

Communicating Brand NaMo

Political parties and politicians have never been easy brands to communicate. By definition, brands must deliver on their promises consistently—and in the context of politicians, these two aspects, delivering on a promise and consistency, are big question marks. One may have the best product or service but it is of no use until the world knows about it. Communication strategy is about getting the marketing message to your target consumer at an optimum cost. A good and well-targeted communication was probably the strength of Modi's campaign. He made a consistent and focused appeal to Indians, yet customized his message differently for the micromarkets. With political parties having a big overlap between their manifestos and objectives, the only significant point of difference seemed to be an individual leading the party. This also gave Modi a well-defined image, enabling people to identify and connect with the brand.

The brand essence and brand positioning

Modi fought the entire campaign on the promise of development and change. He had a team of media and advertising experts who worked diligently for more than a year to build Brand Modi, and packaged, communicated and sold it to the public like any other consumer brand. The team understood that the young Indians (almost 65 per cent of India's population) had a general disdain for politics per se. The communication campaign reflected the mood of the nation and promised a leadership that would give them good governance and a better future.

The BJP also wanted to promote this, as it was keen to change its image from a communal to a more secular party. This shift in strategy gave Modi the opportunity to build on his image as the agent of development and reduce the Hindutva imagery, though he did not discard it altogether. In fact, in his discourse, he referred to Hinduism not as a religion but as a 'way of life', while continually wearing the saffron colour. The colour could be seen on collaterals and as the stage backdrop, but he never let it make its way into his speeches. He communicated to the audience that though he may not wear the symbols of other religions, he definitely respected them all. Modi's delight in dressing well also resonated with a section of the electorate that valued personal growth and progress above politics.

Key communication lesson: *Incorporate your core brand essence loudly or subtly in your communication to build brand equity. Base your campaign on your brand promise or core brand proposition.*

The message strategy

Analysts feel that culturally, Indians have always been quite content to be ruled by a powerful king figure, rather than through the more abstract idea of self-rule. So centralized authority (or even a benevolent dictator) is not anathema to most Indians. The centralization of power and determined authoritarianism could well be seen by today's India as the need of the hour and an attractive antidote to economic stagnation. Hence, the pitch was for 'Modi Sarkar' and not 'BJP Sarkar'. Modi's message was strong and his communication designed to turn people's attention away from the memories of 2002 to the more recent economic transformation of Gujarat and the increasing confidence among the people of the state. The campaign was planned over three layers. The top layer spoke to the nation as a whole and was controlled by Modi himself through his team of volunteers. The second layer was coordinated by party leaders who organized meetings with concerned groups. And the third layer was the RSS and party workers who were involved in last-mile messaging. The strategic message laid emphasis on the party's philosophy and was communicated through *Saugandh*, the BJP anthem to which Modi lent his voice. The tactical messages were aimed to create momentum and get the party the majority in the 2014 election. The message strategy broadly followed an emotional appeal. Modi tried to connect to diverse Indians by addressing their individual concerns and problems. He would empathize with them and draw their attention to similar issues in Gujarat and how his development model worked to solve those. His messages were tailored to specific villages and target groups. While in urban areas, he projected the image of a pro-growth reformist leader, in the Indian hinterland, he spoke about common problems such as corruption, inflation, joblessness, and basic health and sanitation. The final reinforcement of Brand Modi was facilitated by RSS pracharaks and other volunteers through door-to-door campaigning.

Key communication lesson: Brand communication needs to follow a consistent message strategy to communicate the same idea every time. It encapsulates brand positioning and helps in encoding it into a language that is understood by the target group.

The media mix

Brand Modi adopted a 360-degree communication strategy. The campaign used advertising through radio, television (particularly during the Indian Premier League cricket matches), print, posters, hoardings and bus panels, in addition to traditional *nukkad sabhas*, street plays, rallies, social events and public speeches.

Human banners and placards dominated below-the-line (BTL) rally promotions, along with offline activation. Social media and the Internet were used to engage young voters throughout the campaign period. Though the core message was the same—the promise of good governance and development—it was adapted to the media deployed, and customized for each state and urban and rural centre it reached.

Modi left no stone unturned in reaching every nook and cranny of India. Sentiments on social media clearly signalled enthusiasm for Brand Modi.

Modi's brand team leveraged technology for microtargeting even in media-dark rural areas. The BJP found that 30,000 villages of UP and Bihar were media-dark, with no TV, print or radio. They deployed hundreds of mobile vans to reach out to these villages to spread Modi's message. He complemented traditional marketing with equally effective direct marketing initiatives.

Modi attended 437 physical rallies, took part in 5,500 video conferences, 3D rallies and Chai Pe Charcha events. Over a period of six months, the team covered 6 lakh villages, almost all urban and semi-urban households that had television sets, and had a presence on every TV channel, newspaper, radio station, cell phone network and digital media. Modi's campaign reached out to 12 crore first-time voters through his integrated media mix. While the overall ad spend was not available, according to some media reports, the party was estimated to have spent around ₹400 crore on the entire campaign.

Key communication lesson: Integrated marketing communication entails not just employing all mediums but also coordinating them in a way such that they are in synergy with each other. The synergy within mediums helps maximize the returns on media investment.

Social media: creating his 'own' medium

The use of digital media was a strategic decision, as Modi wished to appeal to the young generation, which was frustrated with the Indian political scenario in general and was looking for a change. This generation was seen as hard-working and hopeful, and Modi wanted to make use of this 'hope' in young India. For the same reason, Modi's campaign also tried to motivate everyone to cast their votes to enable the formation of a strong and stable government.

In 2007, YouTube was the first social platform that Modi made tactical use of. Modi's Facebook and Twitter journey commenced two years later, in 2009. He then started blogging and launched his own website. In 2010, Modi's Twitter follower base increased to 1 lakh and, by December 2011, he had over 4 lakh followers, crossing the 1-million mark in October 2012. He has been named the first Indian politician to use Google Hangout and someone who has a mobile app to his name, 'iModi', available on Apple platforms. While campaigning, between January and May 2014, Modi had 7,549,972 likes on his Facebook page and 960,914 people talking about him; on Twitter, he had 4.12 million followers.

Modi's content strategy changed with the changing communication objectives to influence the various stages of the voters' decision-making process. Initially, he intended to communicate his 'brand identity', and hence established his presence on various social media platforms. The content revolved around inspirational quotes, quotes from scriptures and his daily activities. In the second stage of building 'brand interest and associations', Modi's social media presence focused on his past performance, achievements and developments in Gujarat. His followers engaged with the brand by liking or commenting on his posts. While he garnered support, he also invited criticism from the Opposition, the media and a few citizens to create curiosity.

In the final stage of building 'brand preference', Modi shifted his focus to building an emotional connect with his audience. This was the stage where he built his credibility, improved his standing with the audience and amplified his superiority.

Also, there was a notable change in content strategy. Apart from sharing his achievements, he became more vocal about the Opposition and made strong statements to express his opinions. He is perhaps the only celebrity leader to follow others, including his colleagues in the BJP, international leaders, eminent celebrities and a few of his fans and well-wishers as well. That a top public figure followed others back on social media projected him as a 'people's person', and this created an army of advocates for him.

In September 2013, when Modi was declared the prime ministerial candidate from the BJP, he embarked on the final stage of building 'brand resonance', with active campaigning for elections. He integrated social media with ground-level activations and other mediums. The party made extensive use of SMSs, emails, Twitter and Facebook to garner mass support. Modi's comments on social media platforms were picked up by other media for greater discussion, thus generating a buzz in newspapers, radio stations and TV channels. Twitter discussed Modi and his accomplishments in 140 words. Many volunteers were entrusted with the tweeting activities across the board. Modi himself used YouTube to spread his messages. All his speeches and interviews on various platforms, including at political rallies, industry events, management workshops, university sessions and inauguration ceremonies, were uploaded on YouTube. He is also the first Indian politician to reach out to the young audience of India and outside through Google Hangout. For the eighty Lok Sabha seats in UP, special web pages such as NaMoLucknow and NaMoBaghpat were created to start debates and give young India information on BJP volunteers and prevailing issues and controversies. Social media seemed to be the anchor medium for the BJP campaign, aimed at every stage of the voter's decision-making process. It was integrated with other media during various stages of the campaign. It was predicted that social media could influence the election results in 160 constituencies.

Mobile strategy

As per the 2013 data of the Internet and Mobile Association India, the country had 205 million web users but a base of 915.9 million mobile subscribers. The viral messages shared through chat platforms, the India272+ app on Android devices and #Modi4PM donation drives increased visibility and created positive brand associations. Speeches were made available on mobile phones through voice messages for those who could not access the YouTube platform.

Mobile and social media strategy helped Modi engage with people and think of themselves as contributors to India's development. This sense of ownership not only helped bring more and more people to the polling booths but also worked to the BJP's advantage, helping it garner a majority for the party.

> ***Key communication lesson:*** *Owned media, including Facebook, Twitter and YouTube, if used well, can help a brand 'earn' free media platforms. These two together—one with maximum control and the other with least control—can help the brand fulfil various communication objectives through the decision-making process.*

Advertising: leveraging existing mediums for mass reach

To connect with the young audience, Modi's campaign used the creative hook *'Ache din aane wale hain'* (good days are about to come), which captured people's imagination and gave them renewed hope. This was a simple expression that brought hope and positivity and resonated with millions of Indians. In line with this creative idea was the tagline *'Ab ki baar Modi Sarkar'*, created by Soho Square (O&M). This was aimed at the young generation, many of whom were first-time voters who wanted to see India on the path of development. Modi's campaign managers took the nation's problems and connected them with their proposition of change through catchy couplets such as *'Bahut ho gayi mehengayi ki maar, ab ki baar Modi Sarkar; na sahenge naari pe atyachaar, ab ki baar Modi Sarkar'*, which meant 'we have had enough of inflation, this time it is going to be the Modi government; we shall not tolerate persecution of women, this time it is going to be the Modi government'. These became so popular that they were extensively shared over chat and social media platforms.

Punchlines such as *'Janta maaf nahin karegi'* (the public will not forgive) added more buzz to the campaign and fitted well with the theme of hope and positivism. A hard-hitting series of films and animation videos based on campaign themes was also released on multiple platforms with the tagline '*Ab ki baar Modi Sarkar*', and a musical titled *Ache Din Aane Wale Hai, Hum Modi Ji Ko Laane Wale Hai*. This was targeted at the common man, who was finding it difficult to make both ends meet. Other activation ideas such as '*Modi aane wale hain*' and Chai Pe Charcha were customized to communication activities planned around them. All the above propositions bombarded television, newspaper, radio and outdoor space.

> **Key communication lesson**: *The creative hook is the port connecting the brand to the consumer. It helps bring the core brand idea to the target audience in a language that resonates with them. Coordinated and clear advertising built around this creative anchor helps generate word-of-mouth (hummable) messages, creating greater awareness and contributing to the campaign buzz.*

BTL activations and direct marketing: building momentum to create buzz

The curators of the Modi campaign understood the importance of creating a buzz to bring maximum returns to their communication strategy and fulfil Mission 272. This required brand advocates and champions. The first innovative step taken by the managers included building a volunteer army, especially of people under the age of 30—the group that believed in change.

Volunteers were invited through a missed-call initiative at a specific number, and they are the ones who took Modi's vision and promise to every house of the nation.

Reports reveal that there was an average of 10,000 missed calls every day to the specified number and led to more than 130 million interactions. This initiative was also aimed at recruiting volunteers from the interiors of the nation, and hence building a wider network of party workers. Meeting voters in their houses helped the party listen to the concerns of real India and remove any disconnect between intellectual debates and actual conditions. For example, when the party thought that a delay in releasing a manifesto could cost them enormous votes, the party workers found that it was a non-issue for the common man, as he was more concerned about the future and not in written promises.

The campaign taglines were made contemporary, and sometimes controversial, to initiate viral discussions around them. It became 'national timepass' to forward messages and jingles that supported Modi and his campaign. The reach was so wide that even kids were sometimes heard singing campaign taglines.

To draw in the urban youth, the BJP also put up small skits and street plays, or *nukkad nataks*. About 1,200 such acts were performed on themes including price rise and corruption. They formed the NaMo band, which played in malls, college canteens, Barista and Café Coffee Day outlets. The idea of a flash mob for the campaign was aimed to create more word-of-mouth buzz. Music bands took to performing in public places, which usually began with singing popular numbers to attract the crowd and then switched to singing the Modi and BJP theme songs.

All these activities added fuel to the campaign and made it 'hummable', giving it the word-of-mouth popularity that, at the last stage, was spread by the people themselves. The NaMo-branded rotis in Varanasi[11], in line with the Lifebuoy roti-branding during the Kumbh[12], created even more media buzz and visibility.

The 3D studio: reaching out to people

Where Modi couldn't be present himself, he connected with the audience through 3D appearances during rallies, seminars and other events. Through this high-tech virtual medium, Modi got the flexibility to reach out to a greater percentage of the population. Modi's experiment with 3D holograms first happened during the 2012 Gujarat assembly elections, wherein he delivered a speech to fifty-three locations simultaneously. These 3D-hologram rallies were conducted extensively during the election campaign of 2013–14.

Chai Pe Charcha: connecting people

The 'chaiwala' tag given to Modi was soon turned by the BJP into a communication strategy, 'Chai Pe Charcha', to engage people and plan other outreach campaigns around tea meets. The campaign was planned based on the insight that tea in India serves as a social binder and acts as a set-up for both formal and informal discussions. Modi believed that tea stalls were like footpath parliaments, where critical interactions happened. Modi connected electronically with lakhs of supporters and citizens of India through this outreach programme. He would host events from tea stalls in Ahmedabad, which would be relayed across 1,000 more tea stalls in 300 cities.

Modi would appear on a giant screen at these tea stalls with a cup of tea in hand, and discuss issues related to good governance and development. People could interact and ask him their questions using a combination of satellite, DTH, Internet and mobile technology.

Participants were served tea from NaMo-branded pots and in NaMo-branded cups. These events were also played on YouTube. This campaign highlighted two key aspects of Modi's personality: his humble origins and his aspirations. And that was exactly what young India wanted in its leader.

Key communication lesson: While traditional advertising and online activities can spread the message, BTL executions and direct marketing activities help the brand connect with customers by engaging them and making them a contributor. Such activities help in building the customer-brand relationship and generate greater word-of-mouth buzz. And any amount of advertising is smaller than word of mouth, because all communication is ultimately aimed at creating the latter.

The emergence of a cult brand: NaMo

Brand Modi was seen as persistent, insistent and consistent, a combination that gave it compelling and convincing communication. His communication was simple yet strategic, and could find a place in the voters' minds and hearts. Good communication was paired with a good product. Modi's past performance added credibility to his communication strategy. However, in 2019, it remains to be seen how Modi continues to engage the young population of India.

Some scholars have compared the 2014 election with the post-Emergency 1977 election, but according to Ashutosh Varshney, Sol Goldman Professor of International Studies and the Social Sciences at Brown University, 'Unlike 1977, Modi's victory is not simply due to anti-incumbency. He has a message of reconstruction.' Varshney feels that 'India has still not witnessed a national-level mass politician who can make a political claim on behalf of markets and integrate it as part of an election campaign', as Modi did in his election rhetoric.[13]

With the next general election round the corner, news programmes on television and edits and op-eds in newspapers have already started discussing and debating possible outcomes. Ajaz Ashraf from Pakistan, in his article "How Modi's Combative Style Has Resulted in the Battle for 2019 Being Joined So Early in His Tenure", says, 'Prime Minister Narendra Modi's combative style of politics has triggered an informal competition among his political opponents to counter him as ferociously and also become the face of the opposition forces arrayed against the Bharatiya Janata Party.'[14]

Who could possibly be the most effective face to compete with Modi is yet to unfold. Rahul Gandhi has miserably failed to achieve much in positioning himself. The political acumen that should naturally have come to him, with his party having a national presence, seems to be lost. Nitish Kumar and Kejriwal were the other two Modi contenders, who, until 2015, seemed would become the face of the 2019 election, but only time will tell if they can bounce back. With Jayalalithaa's demise, West Bengal's Mamata Banerjee—who vehemently opposed the 8 November demonetization—was brought to centre stage as Modi's prime challenger (both Nitish Kumar and Naveen Patnaik, chief ministers of Bihar and Odisha, respectively, supported demonetization), but the fizz evaporated after a while. In a programme on India News before an invited audience, when someone asked Mulayam Singh Yadav, the patriarch of the SP, when he would become prime minister, he made no bones about saying that he nearly became PM but lost out, and that there seemed no hope now.[15]

With the BJP losing in the Rajasthan, Madhya Pradesh and Chhattisgarh assembly elections held in late 2018; not making a mark in Mizoram, the only Northeastern state where it could not create an impression; and with virtually no presence in Telangana, the narrative seems to have changed. With the Congress forming governments in the three important states and regaining its lost confidence, and with talks about Opposition unity gaining ground, the going may not be easy for the Modi government in the 2019 parliamentary election. Many opinion polls are suggesting that no party may be able to get a clear majority.

In the last chapter, we will discuss the phenomenon of governments being in a constant state of campaigning.

Notes

1. Branding of Politicians—Election 1999, an exploratory research study, was conducted in 1998 by one of the authors, Dr J. Jethwaney, professor, IIMC, along with associate professor Shivaji Sarkar and brand expert Nippun Gupta. Students were trained for the field survey.

2. Ibid
3. Bedi, Rakesh, "Narendra Modi Vs Kejriwal: Two Contrasting Campaign Styles Battle It Out in Varanasi", *The Economic Times*, 9 May 2014
http://economictimes.indiatimes.com/news/politics-and-nation/narendra-modi-vs-kejriwal-two-contrasting-campaign-styles-battle-it-out-in-varanasi/articleshow/34859206.cms
4. "The Lowest Moment in the History of Debates?", *Politico Magazine*, 10 October 2016
https://www.politico.com/magazine/story/2016/10/presidential-debate-2016-donald-trump-hillary-clinton-2016-214342
5. Pande, Shamni, "Just the Right Image", *Business Today*, 8 June 2014
6. Harris, Gardiner, "Campaign for Prime Minister in India Gets Off to Violent Start", *The New York Times*, 17 September 2013
http://www.nytimes.com/2013/09/18/world/asia/indian-vote-off-to-a-violent-start.html?pagewanted%3Dall&_r=0
7. Ibid
8. "The Gujarat Model", *The Economist*, 8 January 2015
http://www.economist.com/news/finance-and-economics/21638147-how-modi-nomics-was-forged-one-indias-most-business-friendly-states
9. Singh, Tavleen, "No More Petitioners: No More Petitioners", *The Indian Express*, 4 May 2014
http://indianexpress.com/article/opinion/columns/no-more-petitioners/#sthash.3fSpb73t.dpuf
10. "LK Advani Calls Narendra Modi an 'Events Manager'", *Deccan Chronicle*, 6 April 2014
http://www.deccanchronicle.com/140406/nation-politics/article/lk-advani-calls-modi-%E2%80%98events-manager%E2%80%99
11. Sengupta, Pallavi, "Cut the Crap! Varanasi Celebrates Modi's Candidature With NaMo Rotis", www.oneindia.com, 8 May 2014
https://www.oneindia.com/india/varanasi-celebrates-modicandidature-with-namo-rotis-1443606.html

12. "HUL's 'Roti Reminder' Lifebuoy Campaign Catches Attention At Kumbh Mela", *The Economic Times*, 8 February 2013
https://economictimes.indiatimes.com/slideshows/advertising-marketing/huls-roti-reminder-lifebuoycampaign-catches-attention-at-kumbh-mela/slideshow/18399577.cms
13. Varshney, Ashutosh, "2014, like 1952", *The Indian Express*, 19 May 2014
http://indianexpress.com/article/opinion/columns/2014-like-1952/
14. Ashraf, Ajaz, "How Modi's Combative Style Has Resulted in the Battle for 2019 Being Joined So Early in His Tenure", *Dawn*, 27 December 2015
https://www.dawn.com/news/1228997
15. India News channel (Hindi), 26 November 2016

7

DISCUSSION: MAPPING THE CHANGES ON INDIA'S POLITICAL LANDSCAPE

> 'In a democracy the poor will have more power than the rich, because there are more of them, and the majority is supreme.'
>
> —ARISTOTLE

India as a nation and Indian elections in the past seven decades or so have surprised and intrigued many. The largest democracy, with more than 800 million voters, out of which a staggering 65 per cent comprises the youth below the age of 35, can make experts go crazy analysing voter behaviour, given the nation's heterogeneity on social, economic, cultural and linguistic parameters. In a country where millions live below the poverty line, in a country low on the honesty meter, where corruption has become a way of life, especially in business, bureaucracy and politics, what really makes it work? Many have spoken of 'jugaad', the art of somehow making things work. When Vajpayee was the prime minister from 1999 to 2004 (the NDA was a coalition of twenty-four parties that lasted a full term), there was a joke making the rounds in social circles that when the visiting former American president, Bill Clinton, asked the Indian prime minister if the US could import jugaad from India, the ever-so-witty Vajpayee replied that if India were to export it, how would it survive?

Indian elections are interesting from many perspectives. India is a nation of festivals. There is always something or the other going on around the year, given the diversity of the country's culture. Election time is no less than a festival running for weeks and months in India, bringing in hectic social, political and economic activities. The parliamentary election every five years in India can be compared to the Maha Kumbh that is celebrated every twelve years. The analogy can be understood and appreciated by only those who have been to the Maha Kumbh. The scenario there looks maddening, with every inch of space occupied by surging humanity. With millions of people converging on the Triveni in Allahabad, the confluence of three rivers—with ascetics in saffron and ash-smeared foreheads, some with mobile phones pressed to their ears; and the media frenzy, complete with publicists and sales promotion teams busy wooing the gullible masses; and the skyline covered in balloons carrying brand messages—the Maha Kumbh is the largest gathering in the world at a given place! India reminds you of something similar to the Maha Kumbh during election time. Every election seals the fate of parties, ideologies and candidates. There are many reasons behind the success and failure of parties and candidates, but the preparation for an election has become a full-time, 24x7, 365-day industry, which includes lakhs of people employed in opinion polling, brand strategy, advertising, publicity, public relations, event management, speech writing and social media.

There are various facets to elections in India, and the way they are conducted has caught the attention of the world, both for positive and negative reasons. In the following paragraphs, we shall critique some of these issues and concerns, which broadly include the following:

- Entry of professional publicists and campaigners
- Governments in constant campaign mode
- Deteriorating standards of political discourse
- Media polarization
- Paid news

Entry of professional publicists and campaigners

Politics is not mathematics and does not always depend on rational reasoning. The pumping of big money into elections from the corporate-politics nexus, and the entry of savvy strategists into politics, for whom ideology is not as important as the art of making possible the impossible, has changed the way elections have been fought, especially since the 1984 parliamentary election, held after the assassination of Indira Gandhi, the serving prime minister.

In an age of post-truth, the Academy Award-winning film *The Candidate*, made in the US in 1972, vindicates the current reality. The film brings into abject focus the promotional dimension of political persuasion. The film is about an idealist who is also a social activist being approached by a professional campaign manager to run for public office. The manager, with his expert team of campaigners, filmmakers and press agents, moulds, packages and markets the candidate through a technically sophisticated mass advertising campaign. The worst fear of the critics of contemporary political campaigns—that unknown candidates through brand positioning and sophisticated campaign strategies can be sold to gullible voters like soaps and detergents in a marketplace—comes true in the closing scene, as the victorious candidate stands bewildered, wondering if he actually is fit for public office. He turns to the campaign manager, a hired professional, who is already looking for a new face to sell, and asks him, 'But what do we do now?' The campaign manager, however, looks through him.

What can explain the success of the most-sought-after spin doctor, nay strategist, Prashant Kishor, who first positioned Nitish Kumar in Bihar, later strategized PM Modi's 2014 parliamentary campaign and then was roped in by the Congress to position Rahul Gandhi—all three leaders with varying political ideologies? No, it was not a hat-trick of being third-time lucky with Rahul Gandhi in the UP election in 2017. The Congress got one of its worse drubbings there. Whatever the strategy, whatever the cunning, the product—the brand—needs to resonate with its core values and a good number of people must believe in it. In fact, in brand parlance, it is often said that a good campaign kills a weak brand faster. However, lo and behold, in the following elections, both in Gujarat and Karnataka, the same Rahul Gandhi who seemed confused and diffident in the Times Now interview in 2014[1] improved his communication skills and the art of rhetoric immensely, connected with the stakeholders and made some strategic tie-ups, improving the party's tally in Gujarat. The Congress formed the government with JD(U) in Karnataka, despite not being in the reckoning.

The whirlwind entry of the AAP in 2012 on the political scene in Delhi took everyone by surprise, especially after the thundering response it received from the electorate! It seemed like a new wave, a paradigm change in politics.

Kejriwal's campaign for the Delhi polls was an example of 'disruptive marketing'. A disruptive strategy positions the brand to match the demand of an emerging market, or reshapes an existing product or service to meet the demand of customers unsatisfied by the current offering. The AAP volunteers went from door to door to identify the deficient areas and crowdsourced ideas. The name, 'Aam Aadmi Party', with the abbreviation AAP, meaning 'you' in Hindi, the quintessential common man, was itself a disruptive tactic, making people the pivot of governance and politics. '*AAP ki Sarkar*', or 'Your government', was used as a metaphor. Everyone was given a 'task' when Kejriwal exhorted the people of Delhi through his radio ads, *'Aap bhi aaiye or apne doston ko bhi le aaiye'* (please come and bring your friends along too). His intent of changing politics forever was perceived as an honest proposition. However, intention always needs to match consistency in performance. The AAP was not able to open its account in the Goa election in 2017 and, despite many political pundits believing that it would form the government in Punjab, the party was much below the Congress, which scored 77 seats, against the AAP, which had to make do with just 21. The expectations were disproven, but for a new entrant to be the leading Opposition party and to score more seats than the incumbent SAD and BJP coalition were achievements in themselves. But because of the expectation that the AAP would win in Punjab, whatever the party got was not seen as an achievement. It only received ridicule in the media, which was rather surprising.

The landslide BJP victory in UP in March 2017 made PM Modi the man of the moment—the man with the Midas touch. The party currently has a pan-Indian appeal, including in the Northeast, the credit for which goes to PM Modi, a feat no leader from the BJP has been able to achieve in the past. Chandan Mitra attributed it to Modi's 'acute sense of politics and his deep-rooted understanding of India's aspirations [which] led to such credibility with the masses', and not just his oratorical skills.[2]

Governments in constant campaign mode

The past few years have witnessed another development—governments, being in constant campaign mode. Here, India has become similar to the US. It is a common saying in the US that the election is over, but it is not yet over. In the Indian context, one has of late seen that as soon as the publicity campaign for an election is over, the result is announced and the winner gets into the saddle—and no time is wasted in preparing for and launching yet another campaign. In their victory speeches after the assembly results in March 2017, both the BJP party president Amit Shah and PM Modi spoke of the 2019 general election and the celebrations in 2022, when Indian Independence reaches its platinum year. Prior to the election in Chhattisgarh, the PR department of the government issued a full-page ad in most of the mainstream national newspapers on 1 October 2018 on the theme, 'Nava Chhattisgarh 2025', unfolding the government's 'India Vision 2025'. It is a different matter that they lost the election to the Congress.

All parties—unfortunately even the Left ones—which tend to make people believe that they have frugal resources, seem to have fallen prey to the practice of showing off in the paid-for media space. Ad campaigns with large pictures of leaders appearing throughout the year in the mainstream media is probably an Indian innovation! The difference, however, is that after winning an election, the party with the majority vote that forms the government spends taxpayers' money on these campaigns! The courts have taken cognizance of this and demanded that parties, not the government, pick up the tab on such campaigns—but the noise pollution continues unabated!

In an interesting article, "Kerala LDF's First 100 days: Ads or Decisions, It's Pinarayi Vijayan Govt", *The Indian Express* commented that after hundred days in office, as on 2 September 2016, the Left government in Kerala, unlike its predecessors the Left Democratic Front (LDF) or the United Democratic Front (UDF), was being identified with one person—Chief Minister Pinarayi Vijayan—to an extent that he was duplicating PM Modi's style of functioning. 'The comparisons became all the sharper,' commented the paper, 'when Vijayan addressed people on radio, similar to the Prime Minister's *Mann Ki Baat*.'[3]

On completion of hundred days, the LDF government issued half-page ads in mainstream media in a pan-India release with the headline, "Now We Have a Government Here", with the picture of a young woman in Western attire carrying a pink bag in one hand and a blue cell phone in the other. Chief Minister Vijayan's passport-size picture appeared with a box alongside and the description 'Pinarayi Vijyan Government 100 days'. The tagline of the ad, 'Change has begun', stood out in white against the red background to denote Left ideology.[4]

'The entire nation today woke up seeing Telangana Chief Minister K. Chandrashekar Rao smiling, as the government of the newest state of the country flooded all the newspapers...with huge advertisements of Telangana Formation Day celebrations and KCR government achievements in these two years,' commented a media website.[5]

In retrospect, both the failed India Shining and Bharat Nirman campaigns by the NDA and the UPA governments, respectively, were launched using thousands of crores of taxpayers' money.

So what could be the possible reason(s) for governments being in this constant campaign mode? One could be of the belief that constant hammering of messages can get them 'top of mind' awareness with relevant stakeholders. The other could be to create a 'feel-good factor' among party workers and voters.

Content of campaigns

The content and emphasis of such campaigns can be broadly divided into three categories:

- Self-congratulatory mode (like 'the hundred days of the Kerala government' ads)
- Testimonial mode (ads like those of the India Shining and Bharat Nirman campaigns)
- Reactive mode against the adversary party's campaign (one

party claiming something and the Opposition questioning that claim)

Full-page ads are now passé—some of the campaigns seen in the recent past are spread across three to four pages. The Telangana and Kerala chief ministers' ads were not restricted to their home states but splashed across mainstream newspapers in various metros as well. There is definitely a tendency towards building personality through ads.

In the past, pictures of prime ministers, chief ministers and other dignitaries in government advertisements would be in passport size, which would be repeated in all the ads all the time. But now, the pictures of political dignitaries come in all sizes and moods, a strategy used in the past few years, especially after the coming of Modi as the Prime Minister and Kejriwal as the Delhi Chief Minister. Others have followed suit.

The completion of the first, second, third and fourth years in office by the BJP government at the centre saw the entire official machinery designing, publishing and printing literature and ads all over the country, besides widely using digital media as well. Blue chip public sector organizations were also roped in to publicize their achievements, with the intent to add to the government's scorecard. It is not uncommon to hear PR and corporate communication managers from such public sector enterprises (PSEs) talking about the 'increasing workload' on them.[6]

The Congress government, in fact, was the one that set the trend in the 1980s. At the centenary celebration of the Congress party in 1985, many PSEs were asked to put up their pavilions in Mumbai, the venue of the celebration, which was visited by the then prime minister, Rajiv Gandhi.

With the Supreme Court's ruling in 2015, that except for the prime minister and the president, no other political personality will appear in ads (which it reviewed later), as per media reports, the

Delhi government shifted its ad focus from print and electronic media to radio by pledging more than ₹500 crore. In a 76-second ad, 'Jo Kaha, So Kiya' (Delivered as promised), Kejriwal talked about his party's prepoll promises and his plans to implement them as envisioned in the presented Delhi Budget.

Modi's *Mann Ki Baat* programme on the AIR, which is aired in Hindi and available in all major Indian languages, is a large platform for a prime minister to be in touch with the populace. Press ads and radio ads preceded his weekly talk, making it an almost everyday affair. He has raised various issues, observations and comments, and shared anecdotes to connect with the audience.

Deteriorating standards of political discourse

It is not uncommon to criticize Opposition candidates in election campaigns, but character assassination and personal attacks have not for long been a tradition in the Indian political discourse. In the past few elections, however, this has changed, and mudslinging has been rampant, especially on social media and prime-time bulletins in news channels. The space for dissenting views has been shrinking. Parties come out with catch phrases against Opposition parties, belittling and often demonizing the other, which one then finds trending on social media and in editorial content. Party spokespersons, in prime-time bulletins, come with an agenda of their own and don't budge from it, no matter what questions are asked to them.

The Gujarat election in December 2017 saw a new low in campaigning. The Gujarat legislative assembly elections in 2017 kept the nation enthralled for weeks. The high-voltage campaigning deviated from the focus on governance and the Gujarat development model into scurrilous mudslinging matches. There was an unprecedented decline in political decorum. Both the Congress and the BJP trivialized the national discourse with rabble-rousing politics. The Opposition capitalized on public anger over losses caused by the twin effects of demonetization and the implementation of the goods and services tax (GST). The simmering discontent amongst Gujarat's resourceful Patidar community was another burning issue, with huge political ramifications. The ruling BJP government was not entirely on strong political turf. The party was battling the anti-incumbency factor from both the centre and the state, as well as the overall slump in growth, the agrarian crisis and subdued business sentiments. This was not an ideal situation for a state known for its mercantile character. Initially, the BJP took the Congress lightly, but soon realized its mistake and galvanized its entire might behind the election campaign. To its credit, the BJP managed to control the narratives around the political discourse the entire stretch of electioneering in Gujarat, but it soon realized that its election agenda had fallen short of people's expectations and therefore reverted to its tried-and-tested ethnopolitical approach. This altered the political discourse and the Congress had to jettison its long-standing position of religious neutrality and project a mild religious image, termed by the media as soft Hindutva. Rahul Gandhi, the then Congress vice-president began visiting temples to drive home that image. There was a wide chasm between the brand of politics displayed by the parties and the actual issues on the ground. This bankruptcy of issues brought about a marked belligerence in the tone and tenor of political parties in Gujarat. As a result, the state witnessed an unprecedented decline in the manner in which political parties conducted their campaigns. Here are some instances:

- Throwing all sense of political decorum to the wind, the Congress party went all out to target the BJP in a no-holds-barred attack. Rahul Gandhi went hammer and tongs at the Gujarat model. He accused Modi of running a 'suit-boot ki sarkar', or 'a government for the rich', which only catered to

the needs of big businesses. This came on the heels of the controversy around Modi's penchant for luxuries, including prohibitively expensive monogrammed pinstriped suits.
- The Congress accused the ECI of acting like a 'frontal organization of the BJP' for not stopping Modi's 'roadshow' in Ahmedabad when voting was in its second phase.[7]
- Hardik Patel, who led the Patidar community, blamed the BJP's 'dirty politics' for the alleged sex videos of him that surfaced on social media.[8]

'The language used was atrocious and toxic in the Gujarat elections. "*Neech*" was a terrible comment, but what the prime minister said about Pakistan and Dr Manmohan Singh was equally undesirable,' commented Sagarika Ghose on NDTV Studio, analysing the Gujarat election on 18 December 2017.

BJP president Amit Shah, in his press conference after winning Gujarat, criticized the Congress for 'playing with caste politics'. To quote him, '*Chunav jitney ki lallak mein jis tarah samvad ka star neeche gira uss ka kuchch toh aasar hota hai*', meaning, 'In a bid to win elections, the standard of political discourse went so low that it had to have some impact'.[9] As a prelude to the Madhya Pradesh election, the BJP president did not shy away from calling alleged illegal immigrants from Bangladesh 'termites'. To quote from *The Hindu*, addressing a rally at Ratlam in poll-bound Madhya Pradesh, Shah again described illegal immigrants as 'termites' and promised to 'drive them out'.[10] *The Indian Express* in its editorial "Hard and Narrow" commented on Shah's reference to 'illegal Bangladeshis' thus: 'It is a signal, an intimation of the tone and content of the electioneering for 2019 that may have already begun. It is a warning that the campaign will be more stripped of compassion and civility than is already anticipated and feared.'[11] The comment came in the wake of Shah's speech, in which he said '*chun chun ke nikalenge*', meaning, 'we will expel them one by one', for alleged Bangladeshis in Assam, while at the same time welcoming Hindus from Bangladesh.

In retrospect, Kejriwal's 9.48-minute video addressing his party MLAs, volunteers and the common man, released via his social media platform on 26 July 2016, set new paradigms in political communication, albeit with dangerous consequences.

In the video, he is seen talking about *'daman ka chakr'*, or 'the axis of domination', by the central government agencies against his party and MLAs. To quote him, 'I want to understand it… there would be some mastermind. Is it Amit Shah, Modiji, PMO? They are all together… Why are they doing it? I am not able to understand the reason. There is negative perception among the people.' He went on to say, *'Modiji bahut bokhlaye hue hein. Bahut gusse mein hein. Isska koi logic nahin'*, meaning, 'Modiji is very upset. He is very angry. This has no logic.' He added that all those AAP MLAs who were arrested were released because the probing agencies could not find evidence against them. The PM, he said, was upset because people felt that the Delhi government was doing well. Calling the PM 'the king', he said, *'Agar iss desh ka raja bokhlahat mein gusse se nirnay le rahe hei, toh ye desh ke liye bahut bura hai. Yeh desh ke liye bahut khatre ki baat hai,'* meaning, 'If the king of the country is taking decisions when he is upset, it is going to be bad for the country. It is something dangerous.'[12]

All the major news channels covered the video, showing snatches of it to viewers. NDTV aired a headline, '"The PM can get him killed," says Delhi CM in his video.' The video showed him saying, *'Unhone ek ek kar ke harr ek party ko kuchal diya. Congress ki himmat nahin hai ab kuch kehene ki. Dalito ko kuchal diya, Rohith Vemula ko kuchal diya, kisano ko kuchal diya. Hamare peechhe CBI ko sab ko chhod diya, income tax ko chhod diya, police ko chhod diya, par hamare hossle ko nahin kuchal sake. Aane wale samay mein yeh daman aur bura hone wala hai. Yeh hum sab ko marva sakte hein. Mujhe bhi marva sakte hein. Jail toh sab ko jaana pad sakta hei. Sab sath raho.'*

Roughly translated, Kejriwal said that one by one, the farmers and the Dalits have been crushed. The CBI, he said, is out for the AAP's blood, and in times to come, it would only get worse. He then referred to the Congress, saying it had no guts to question what was happening. Finally, he said that everybody, including him, could be killed.

When Kejriwal posted the video on Facebook and Twitter, it went viral on 26 July 2016. Whether what he said was right is for history and posterity to judge, but there is no denying that the standard of public discourse has deplorably fallen. The Delhi Chief Minister has 14.3 million Twitter followers.[13] Imagine the kind of multiplier impact it could have. PM Modi has more than 45 million Twitter followers, which is the second highest for anyone in the world, preceded only by former US president Barack Obama. Therefore, it is incumbent on political leaders to use caution and not arouse passions for narrow political gains.

In its editorial "The PM's Tongue", the weekly magazine *Outlook* commented that the PM was using foreign soil to express his indignation towards the 'previous Congress government' and its leaders, and that 'we the people' was not the right strategy. 'But even so masterful a speaker needs to remind himself—or needs to be reminded—that he is the nation's prime minister, not some lowly rabble-rouser, and that moment is now,' the magazine said. Quoting Amitabh Bachchan's iconic dialogue from *Amar Akbar Anthony*—'You see, the whole country of the system is juxtapositioned by the haemoglobin in the atmosphere because you are a sophisticated rhetorician intoxicated by the exuberance of your own verbosity'—the editorial exhorted the PM thus, 'Reining in the rhetoric would certainly be a good first step.'[14]

This makes one ask in disgust: In which direction are India's political campaigns headed?

Interestingly, while addressing the BJP's national executive meeting in Allahabad on 14 June 2016, the PM, as reported by the media, said, 'The people of the country cannot be made happy by just sloganeering. The time for sloganeering is over. They want to see the country strengthened.'[15]

Now let us look at some of the paid advertising campaigns of the BJP and the AAP between 2014 and 2016 to understand the malaise. When contesting the Delhi elections for the first time, the AAP came up with an ad, with pictures of Kejriwal and the then chief minister Sheila Dixit, and the copy, '*Iss baar bhi diya beimano ko vote, toh mahilaon ka hota rahega balatakar*', meaning, 'If you vote for the corrupt this time too, then women will continue to get raped'. The pictures had the captions 'Honest' and 'Corrupt', respectively.

When Kejriwal threatened dharna, the BJP came up with the ad, 'If you don't listen to me, I am going to disrupt the Republic Day function', making fun of him.

When the AAP released an ad showing the number of corrupt officers who had been arrested—'The corrupt will not be spared. 35 arrested, 120 suspended'—the BJP instantly responded with rejoinder ads on big billboards—'Mr Liar, tell us the names of the persons arrested.' These are just a couple of examples of the deteriorating public discourse and the lack of respect among parties.

Religious polarization

Appeasing minorities may have been a strategy with the left-of-centre parties for a long time, but after 2014, the issues of Hindutva and 'who is a better Hindu'—so long only the BJP's prerogative—seemed to have percolated into the Congress as well, drawing sharp criticism from the BJP. Rahul Gandhi's many temple visits during his campaigning in Gujarat and Karnataka, his Kailash Mansarovar Yatra and his wearing of the sacred Hindu thread, or 'janeu', were perceived as threats to the BJP's Hindutva positioning, and raised the ire of the party.

Rahul Gandhi, in the meantime,, seemed to have gone through

his real political baptism in 2017 during the Gujarat election, as he appeared more articulate and suave, unlike his earlier fumbling persona. Analysts believe that due to the new caste coalitions and three young leaders joining hands with the Congress—including 24-year-old Hardik Patel, who led the formidable Patidar Andolan, or the Patidar reservation agitation, demanding quota reservation for the Patel community in government educational institutions and jobs—the election was no less than a war. An analyst on a Hindi channel called it *'naak ki ladaai'*, meaning 'the battle for retaining reputation'.

On 9 December, after the first phase was over, and the BJP leadership thought that the fight could get tougher, PM Modi upped his rhetoric and said things at public meetings which, many felt, were unbecoming of a prime minister. He alleged that a conspiracy was being hatched at a meeting held during Congress member Mani Shankar Aiyar's dinner party, attended by former prime minister Manmohan Singh, a former Army chief and a former Pakistani diplomat and minister. He also speculated that the meeting was convened to propose Ahmed Patel as the chief minister of Gujarat. Manmohan Singh, seemingly hurt at the allegations, released a press statement and video in response to Modi's remarks. This came after Aiyar called Modi a *'neech kism ka aadmi'*, or a low life. It was taken as a caste slur. The Congress immediately suspended Aiyar, implying, at least for the general public, that his actions were unbecoming of a Congressman. The PM's suspicions of a conspiracy theory, however, did not sit well with the common man. To quote the vice chancellor of the Ashoka University, Pratap Bhanu Mehta, in an opinion piece in *The Indian Express*, 'The Prime Minister, instead of navigating constitutional values, ordinary decencies of discourse and civility, to safe harbour, is now bent on creating new storms. Whether he wins or loses in Gujarat, he is spreading a poison from which Indian politics will find it hard to recover for quite some time.'[16]

Media polarization

Looking at the media sociology, theoretically it is not impossible for media houses to have varying political inclinations. However, there was a time in India when journalists, despite their political inclinations, would not align themselves publicly with any particular political party. However, all this changed a few decades back, when journalists started getting Rajya Sabha nominations from parties that they were sympathetic to in their articles. M.J. Akbar, Pritish Nandy, Balbir Punj, Kumar Ketkar and Rajiv Shukla are a few such names. 'Every time a journalist or a media owner is nominated to the Rajya Sabha, it evokes a passing bout of hand-wringing over journalistic independence,' media columnist Sevanti Ninan wrote in a column.[17] Rajdeep Sardesai echoed her views in his blog.

Challenging the Media, a seminar organized by the Editors' Guild in 2012, had many eminent journalists talking about various issues related to obstacles and trials the media faced in India.

Veteran journalist Shekhar Gupta ridiculed media persons on accepting nominations to the Rajya Sabha or finding a place on government committees. 'The problem is with senior journalists and editors embracing government all the time... Accepting Rajya Sabha nominations, government committees, it's criminal!' he rued.[18] Raghav Bahl echoed Gupta's sentiments when he said, 'While in the Nineties we used to approach government handouts with scepticism, it is not so any more. We seem to be purveying a government-is-god kind of stance, even when the government line is flawed... The CAG report falls squarely in this category.' While Bahl attributed the media's mistakes to 'inexperience and youthful energy', Gupta said it was the fault of 'senior and famous editors and anchors'.[19]

Paid news

One of the maladies plaguing the Indian media today is the paid news syndrome. Both mainstream and regional media are guilty of entertaining paid news, with a few honourable exceptions. Election time is 'windfall season' for media houses. Veteran journalist Mrinal Pande, while speaking at a media seminar, narrated how the CEO of a big media house in Delhi told her that the Hindi media had performed better than the English media in earning huge revenues, thanks to election time!

S.Y. Quraishi, former Chief Election Commissioner, recounted the cases on paid news—121 cases during the Bihar election and 250 when polls were held in Tamil Nadu, West Bengal, Kerala, Assam and Puducherry. In the 2012 elections in UP and other states, 766 complaints about paid news were received, in which notices were issued to 581 because prima facie cases were established. He also said that there were admissions in 253 of the cases. The ECI, he shared, had recommended that the government make paid news a cognizable offence.

One of the key players in sustaining democracy in India has undoubtedly been the media. Its role during election time has always been crucial. An objective media can function as a watchdog. The reach of the media in India has been phenomenal, so much so that even as print media readership has been decreasing in fully literate societies, in India there has been a surge in circulation and readership. The quality of content, however, has been a constant source of concern. The rising cost of maintaining media empires and increasing competition have given rise to the paid news phenomenon, a malady that needs to be addressed before it gets entrenched in media ethos. It is high time the authorities treated paid news as a criminal offence.

The biggest culprit, many feel, is the use of big and unaccounted-for money from corporate houses in political campaigns. It is an open secret that parties and candidates spend huge sums on paid advertising, which is usually thousands of times more than the ECI ceiling, but those who are supposed to question this turn a blind eye to it. The corporate-politics nexus is yet another area that needs immediate addressing.

In summation, one can say that the Indian democracy, despite its flaws, is a great story that needs to not only be studied but emulated by fledgling democracies. The issues flagged above, however, are crucial and need to be addressed before it is too late. This book, it is hoped, will give readers an overall picture of India and its democracy, its media and its election processes, rich in both their dynamics and undercurrents.

Notes

1. *Frankly Speaking,* Arnab Goswami with Rahul Gandhi, Times Now, 24 January 2014
   https://www.youtube.com/watch?v=xB_eWW5ttaM
2. Mitra, Chandan, "Man of Destiny", *The Pioneer,* 12 March 2017. Chandan Mitra, the BJP Rajya Sabha MP, resigned from the BJP and has incidentally joined Trinamool Congress, headed by Mamata Banerjee, the West Bengal Chief Minister.
   https://indianexpress.com/article/india/former-bjp-lawmaker-chandan-mitra-joins-trinamool-congress/
3. Philip, Shaju, "Kerala LDF's First 100 days: Ads or Decisions, It's Pinarayi Vijayan Govt", *The Indian Express,* 2 September 2016
4. Ibid
5. https://www.mirchi9.com/politics/nation-wakes-kcr-smile/
6. One of the authors who worked in a PSE was privy to it.
7. "Gujarat Assembly Elections 2017: 10 Controversies During Poll Campaign", Oneindia.com, 18 December 2017
   https://www.oneindia.com/india/gujarat-assembly-elections-2017-10-controversies-during-poll-campaign-2604111.html

8. "Sex CD Leak: Hardik Patel Says It's BJP's 'Dirty Politics'", *Business Standard*, 14 November 2017
   https://www.business-standard.com/article/politics/sex-cd-leak-hardik-patel-says-it-s-bjp-s-dirty-politics-117111301238_1.html
9. Sagarika Ghose on NDTV Studio, analysing the Gujarat election on 18 December 2017, 4.14 p.m.
10. "Shah Again Calls Illegal Immigrants 'Termites'", *The Hindu*, 7 October 2018
    https://www.thehindu.com/todays-paper/shah-again-calls-illegal-immigrants-termites/article25147245.ece
11. "Hard and Narrow", *The Indian Express*, 13 September 2018
12. https://www.navodayatimes.in/news/delhi-ncr/kejriwal-slam-modi-government/11699/?webSyncID=63e78849-b65b-c90a-b29d-0452c2dc9845&sessionGUID=770a5516-c338-47aa-83de-1d9890483779
13. https://twitter.com/arvindkejriwal (Accessed on 4 January 2019)
14. "The PM's Tongue", *Outlook*, 6 June 2016, Vol.LVI, No.22 p.3
15. Hebbar, Nistula, "Time for Sloganeering Over, PM Tells Party Men", *The Hindu*, 15 June 2016
16. Mehta, Pratap B., "Power and Insecurity", *The Indian Express*, 13 December 2017
    https://indianexpress.com/article/opinion/columns/power-and-insecurity-prime-minister-narendra-modi-gujarat-elections-communal-innuendos-4979986/
17. Ninan, Sevanti, "Rajya Sabha Polls: Keeping Politics and Journalism Apart Is the Rule, But Exceptions Are Increasing", Scroll.in, 14 March 2018
    https://scroll.in/article/871923/rajya-sabha-pollskeeping-politics-and-journalism-apart-is-the-rule-but-exceptionsare-increasing
18. Manocha, Aastha, "Challenging the Media", Newslaundry.com, 13 July 2012
    https://www.newslaundry.com/2012/07/13/challenging-the-media
19. Ibid

ACKNOWLEDGMENTS

Writing this book was truly a labour of love for both of us—one a media academic and election researcher for long, and the other an election campaign strategist. After the sixteenth general election, a casual discussion between the two of us at the Indian Institute of Mass Communication (IIMC), where one was a professor and the other a visiting faculty, resulted in shaping the contents of the book, *When India Votes: The Dynamics of Successful Election Campaigning*.

First and foremost on our list of gratitude is Mr Kapish Mehra, Managing Director, Rupa Publications, for strategically timing the publishing schedule and agreeing to get the book peer-reviewed at our instance. We felt that as the book hopefully would be of interest to the academic fraternity, besides the general reader who evinces interest in election campaigns, it would only be prudent to run it through the requisite academic rigour.

Things were changing so dramatically and so fast on the Indian political turf, with election after election bringing newer insights in 2017–2018, that after submitting the manuscript, we kept revising the chapters to provide newer aspects of election campaigning to the readers.

We wish to thank the team led by Rudra Narayan Sharma, commissioning editor, and editors Nishtha Kapil and Ujjaini Dasgupta for their diligence, cordiality and, above all, patience.

We would also like to thank our respective colleagues at IIMC and the Institute for Studies in Industrial Development (ISID), and Adfactors PR for our long discussions and debates on election discourse and deconstruction of campaigning styles of various players from time to time.

Dr Anand Pradhan, a well-known media academic, election analyst and colleague at IIMC, deserves our special mention.

Thanks are also due to Professor S.K. Goyal, Dr M.R. Murthy and Professor Seema Goyal at ISID, and Madan Bahal and Rajesh Chaturvedi at Adfactors PR for their wholehearted support.

We can't thank enough Sunita Palita for painstakingly previewing the manuscript before it was handed over to the publisher.

Families are always the cornerstone of all human accomplishments and just a 'thank you' shall not suffice!

Jaishri Jethwaney
Samir Kapur

INDEX

Aam Aadmi Party (AAP), 17, 82, 89, 109, 183–84, 191, 193
Adityanath, Yogi, 60
Adult franchise, 73. *See also* Ambedkar, B.R.; Simon Commission
Advani, L.K., 119, 124, 126, 130, 164
Agenda-setting theory, 9–10
Aiyar, Mani Shankar, 194
Akbar, M.J., 99, 195
Al Jazeera, 62
All India Anna Dravida Munnetra Kazhagam (AIADMK), 91, 125, 128
Amar Ujala, 57
Ambani, Anil, 149
Ambani, Mukesh, 149
Ambedkar, B.R., 73, 107, 109
Americanization of elections, 2, 56, 108, 135
Andrade, Meylin K. Menjivar, 38
Anti-incumbency, 42, 176, 189
Aristotle, 105
Ashraf, Ajaz, 176
Asian News International (ANI), 53
Asom Gana Parishad, 117
Assange, Julian, 38
Atre, P.K., 108

Bahl, Raghav, 195
Bahujan Samaj Party (BSP), 61, 87, 89–90, 99, 125, 128, 132, 135
Bal Narendra (Modi as a child), 144, 155
Balsara, Sam, 154
Banerjee, Mamata, 145, 156, 177
Baran, Stanley J., 6, 85
Basu, Jyoti, 145
Beef controversy, 42

Bennet, Lance, 51
Bhagat, Chetan, 43
Bharat Nirman campaign, 88, 134, 137, 163, 186
Bharatiya Janata Party (BJP), 17, 30, 42, 51–52, 60–61, 64, 74, 82, 87, 89–90, 92–94, 96–102, 115–20, 122–25, 127–37, 146–50, 154, 156–58, 161–62, 164–68, 170–71, 174–77, 184–85, 187–90, 193–94
  2014 general election performance, 90, 94
  Bharat Nirman campaign, 88, 134, 137, 163, 186
  branding of Modi, 148
  cadre-based workforce, 117
  campaign, 2014, 164–75
    Chai Pe Charcha, 175
    3D studio, 174–75
    advertising, 172–73
    brand essence, 166
    brand positioning, 166
    BTL activations, 173–74
    communicating brand NaMo, 165–66
    direct marketing, 173–74
    media mix, 168–69
    message strategy, 167–68
    mobile strategy, 171–72
    PR to build credibility, 164–65
    social media, 169–70
  landslide victory in Uttar Pradesh, 184
  Modi campaign, 100–2
  polarized the Hindus votes, 92
  rath yatra, 119
  religious solidarity, 92

step-by-step ascent, 108
tagline for Atal Bihari Vajpayee, 141
'Videshi vs. Swadeshi theme', 128
Bhartiya Pravasi Sammelan, 128
Bhindranwale, 110. *See also* Khalistan issue
Bhushan, Sandeep, 39
Biju Janata Dal (BJD), 91
Bird Wathcer's Digest, 80
Biswas, Aindrila, 41
Bofors, 116, 118, 122, 131. *See also* Gandhi, Rajiv
Brand identity, 142–43, 145, 170
six facets define, 143
Brand management, 141
Brand Modi, 144, 147, 156–57, 160, 162, 164, 166, 168, 176
360-degree communication strategy, 168
diverting public attention, 156
making of, 147–51
promise of, 148
'brand resonance', 170
Business India, 123

CAG report, 195
Campaigning
Ad campaign of Congress, 112–14
BJP campaign, 122–2
door-to-door, 41, 108, 168
in earlier times, 106
election campaign 1989, 116–20
election campaign 1991, 120–22
election campaign 1996, 125–28
election campaign 1999, 128–29
election campaign 2004, 129–32
election campaign 2009, 133–35
general election 1984, 111–16
India Shining, 130
Jaago Re (Wake Up), 84
outdoor media, 108
parliamentary election of 2009, 132–33
punchlines, 172–73
rallies, 108
taglines, 174
voice-over technique, 133

Westernization of, 17
Westminster democracy style, 134
Campbell, Angus, 76
Caste-based voting, 90
Center for Media Studies (CMS), 64
Central Bureau of Investigation (CBI), 127, 191–92
Centre for the Study of Developing Societies (CSDS), 90–91
Chai Pe Charcha, 154, 160, 169, 175
Chavan, Ashok, 57
Chidambaram, P., 163
Childs, Harwood L., 3
Chomsky, Noam, 50
Citizen journalists, 26
Citizens for Accountable Governance (CAG), 154
Clinton, Bill, 180
Cohen, Bernard S., 10
Commonwealth Games, 133
Communist Party of India (CPI), 107, 120, 129
Confederation of Indian Industry (CII), 82
Congress Socialist Party, 107
Constant campaign mode, 184–88
Corporate-politics nexus, 182, 197

Dainik Jagran, 57
Das, Akhilesh, 61
Data fudging, 87
Davis, Dennis K., 85
DellaVigna, Stefano, 37
Democracy, interdependence of, 6–12
Demonetization, 42–43, 177, 189
Desai, Santosh, 52, 87
Deve Gowda, H.D., 127
Digital media, 21, 30, 81–82, 154, 169, 187
Dikshit, Sandeep, 61
Disruptive marketing, 183. *See also* Kejriwal, Arvind
Dixit, Sheila, 193
Dravida Munnetra Kazhagam (DMK), 117, 128
Dutt, Sunil, 131
Dynastic politicians with criminal

records, 93

Economic & Political Weekly, 80
The Economic Times, 124, 147
The Economist, 163, 165
Editors Guild, 56, 195
Election campaign. *See* Campaigning
Election Commission of India (ECI), 17
   model code of conduct, 133, 137
   violation the model code of conduct, 133
Election manifestos, 123
Electronic Voting Machines (EVMs), 89
Emergency, 27, 110, 136, 176
Ethical Journalism Network, 53
Ethical violations, guilty of, 57
Exit polls, 63–64, 87

Facebook, 30, 41, 79–80, 151, 159, 170–72, 192
Feel-good factor, 186
'Fenku', 106, 151. *See* also Modi, Narendra
FICCI-KPMG-Indian Media and Entertainment Industry Report, 23, 28
The Financial Express, 51
'First past the post', 131
First World War, 6
Flanigan, William H., 76
Fodder scam, 127. *See also* Yadav, Lalu Prasad
Folk media, 34–36
Folk theatre, 36
Forcible sterilization programme, 136. *See also* Emergency
Foreign direct investment (FDI), 27
Forward Bloc, 132
Framing theory, 38
Freedom of media, 4
Freedom of press, 4, 16, 27, 58
Freedom of speech, 4–5, 136

Gandhi, Indira, 27, 107, 109–12, 115, 130, 135–36, 141, 182

Gandhi, Maneka, 92
Gandhi, Rahul, 43, 61, 64, 106, 148, 150–51, 161, 163, 176, 183, 189, 193–94
   improved communication skills, 183
   interview to Arnab Goswami, 161
   Kailash Mansarovar Yatra, 193
   news channels coverage, 64
   political baptism, 194
   as Shehzada, 106, 163
   temple visits, 189, 193
Gandhi, Rajiv, 111–12, 115–20, 122, 124, 126, 128, 131, 187
Gandhi, Sonia, 92, 128–31, 144–46, 163
   foreign-origin issue, 128–30
   run the govt. through remote, 131
Gandhi, Varun, 92
'Garibi Hatao', 136. *See also* Gandhi, Indira
'Gatekeeper', 13
General election, 1984, 111
Ghose, Sagarika, 190
Godhra riots, 147–48, 163
Goebbels, Joseph, 79
Goffman, Erving, 38
Golden Temple, 110, 113
Goods and services tax (GST), 189
Goswami, Arnab, 161
Goyal, Piyush, 154
The Guardian, 59, 131–32
Guha, Ramachandra, 108
'Gujarat model' of governance, 144
Gujarat riots (2002), 144, 162
Gujral, I.K., 127
Gujral, Naresh, 61
Gupta, Dipankar, 98
Gupta, Shekhar, 195

Harrop, Martin, 11–12
Hasan, Zoya, 39
Haselmayer, Martin, 13
Hegel, Georg Wilhelm Friedrich, 15
'Helpless audiences', 7
Herman, Edward S., 50
Hindu vote consolidation, 90
The Hindu, 42, 53, 57, 59, 190

Hindu-Muslim polarization, 90
Hindustan Times, 42
Hindutava agenda, 145
Hitler, 79, 163
Hooda, Bhupinder Singh, 60
'Horse race' aspect of election, 87
Housing Census data, 75
Human banners, 168. *See also* Campaigning
Hutchins Commission, 16

Identity prism, 143
Identity-based concerns, 93
'iModi', mobile app, 170
India After Gandhi, 108
India Shining campaign, 88, 130, 132, 134, 137, 152, 163, 186
India Today, 126, 132, 165
Indian Constitution, 27, 73
The Indian Express, 27, 123, 185, 190, 194
Indian Institute of Mass Communication, 145
Indian National Congress. *See* Congress
Indian Readership Survey (IRS), 23
Informing the News, 51
Ingle, Nikhil, 41
Instagram, 80
Institutional mechanisms, 58
'Internal Emergency', 10. *See also* Emergency
Internet access, 21
Internet and Mobile Association India, 171
Interpersonal communication, 21, 41
'Intolerance', 42
Introduction to Mass Communication, 6
An Introduction to Public Opinion, 3

jaagore.com, 84
Jain Hawala case, 126
Jaitley, Arun, 61, 147
Jana Sangh, 107–9
Janata Dal, 90, 116–19, 125–27
 manifesto, 126
Janata Dal (United), 90, 128, 183

Janata Party, 108, 110, 116
Jat agitation (2016), 119
Jawaharlal Nehru University (JNU) sedition story, 42–43
Jayalalithaa, J., 128, 145, 156
Jenson & Nicholson, 112
Joshi, Murali Manohar, 164
Joshi, Prasoon, 154
Journalistic objectivity, 55

Kajrolkar, Narayan Sadoba, 109
Kapferer, Jean-Noël, 142
 brand identity model, 144
Kaplan, Ethan, 37
Kargil war, 128–29
Kejriwal, Arvind, 17, 64, 89, 147, 177, 183–84, 187–88, 191–93
 media coverage, 64
Ketkar, Kumar, 195
Khalistan issue, 111
Khare, Harish, 115
Khurana, Madan Lal, 115
Kisan Mazdoor Praja Parishad, 107
Kishor, Prashant, 154, 183
Klapper, Joseph, 8–9
Knowledge-based journalism, 51
Kohli, Nalin, 147
Kotler, Philip, 159
Kripalani, Acharya, 107
Kumar, Nitish, 156, 177, 183

Lal, Devi, 119
Lasswell, Harold Dwight, 7
Lazarsfeld, Paul Felix, 7
Left Democratic Front (LDF), 185
Leftist, 5
Lewin, Kurt, 13
Liberalization of the economy, 128
Lincoln, Abraham, 72
Lippmann, Walter, 5, 10
Locke, John, 15
Lohia, Manohar, 107
Lokniti, 100

Madison, James, 20
Maha Kumbh, 182
Malhotra, Vijay Kumar, 115

Malini, Hema, 131
Mandal Commission report, 118–19.
    See also Singh, V.P.
Manifestos, economic content, 123
Manufacturing Consent, 50
Marketing and Research Group (MARG), 88
Marketing Management, 159
Marx, Karl, 15
Mass media
    attributes, 2–3
    gatekeeping function, 13–14
    impact on voting behaviour, 39–43
    radical model of voting, 11
    strengths and weaknesses, 30–34
        cinema, 33
        internet/digital media, 33
        local/regional newspapers, 31
        magazines, 32
        mobile phones and SMS, 34
        outdoor (posters, billboards, hoarding), 33
        press, 31
        radio, 32
        television, 32
    as a tool of propaganda, 6
Mass society theory, 85
(mass) dissemination of ideas, 79
'mass' in mass communication, 78–80
'*Maut ka saudagar*'. *See* Modi, Narendra
Mayawati, 89, 145
McCann Worldgroup, 154
McCombs, Max, 9
McLuhan, Marshall, 6
McQuail, Denis, 2
Media
    bias, impact on politics, 37–38
    content, 49
    functions of public enlightenment, 5
    influence on the audience as voters, 85–86
    mandatory disclosures by, 44
    objectivity, 53–57, 65
    polarization, 195–96
    and politics, 4–6
    reinforcement theory, 8
Media audiences, anatomy of, 80–83

audience fragmentation, 81
audience in marketing terms, 82–83
mass audience, 80
niche audience, 80–81
tech-savvy audience, 81–82
Media management company. *See* Orchid; Perfect Relations
Medianet, 25
Mehta, Vinod, 55
Meyer, Thomas S., 13
Mill, John Stuart, 15
Milton, John, 15
Minimal effect theory, 9
Minimum government-maximum governance, 148
Mitra, Chandan, 184
MNREGA, 134, 153
Mobile-phone advertising, 82
Model code of conduct, 133, 137
Modi, Narendra
    437 physical rallies, 169
    campaign for good governance, 162
    campaign managers, 172
    content strategy, 170
    election campaign, 146
    emergence on the national electoral scene, 141–42
    Facebook journey, 169
    functioning style, 185
    image as self-made, 157
    Mann Ki Baat, 185
    marketing team, 150
    penchant for luxuries, 190
    public outreach programme and strategy, 146–47
    'roadshow', 190
    at Shri Ram College of Commerce (SRCC), 149
    social media presence, 170
    speech at New York, 61
    storytelling style, 150
    support and advocacy of corporate leaders, 151
    Twitter follower base, 169
    vision and promise, 173
Mookerjee, Shyama Prasad, 107
Moorthi, Y.L.R., 157

Motilal Nehru Committee, 73
'Mr Clean'. *See* Gandhi, Rajiv
Mullen, Lawrence J., 38

Naidu, Chandra Babu, 145
NaMo emergence of brand, 176–77
NaMo versus RaGa, 106
Nandy, Pritish, 195
Narayan, Jayaprakash, 22, 107, 110
National Conference, 128
National Democratic Alliance (NDA), 100, 128–32, 153, 180, 186
National Democratic Front, 128
National Election Study (NES), 101
National Front, 117–18, 122, 124–127
Nationalist Congress Party, 128
Navbharat Times, 124
Nehru, Arun, 111–12
Nehru-Gandhi dynasty, 189
Nehru, Jawaharlal, 106–7, 109, 135
The New York Times, 161, 165
Newspaper trends, 22–23
Ninan, Sevanti, 195
Ninan, T.N., 124
Nukkad nataks, 174

Obama, Barack, 192
Objectivity, lack of, 54–55
Ogilvy & Mather, 154
Onion peel model, 158–60
  community meaning, 159
  cultural meaning, 158–59
  individual meaning, 159–60
Operation Blue Star, 110. *See also* Gandhi, Indira; Khalistan issue
'Opinion leader', 8
Orchid, 131
Outlook, 59–60, 192

Paid advertising campaigns, 193
Paid-for (advertising), 21
'Paid media' coverage, 12, 21, 56
Paid news, 17, 21, 25, 40, 53, 56, 58–61, 65–67, 137, 182, 196–97
Paid surveys, 65
Pande, Mrinal, 196
Pandey, Piyush, 154

'Pappu'. *See* Gandhi, Rahul
Parliamentary election (2009), 132–33
Party identification model, 10–11
Patel, Hardik, 190, 194
Patidar Andolan, 194. *See also* Patel, Hardik
Patnaik, Naveen, 177
Patterson, Thomas E., 51
Pawar, Sharad, 128
Perfect Relations, 131
Personality-driven campaign, presidential style, 134
'Policy paralysis', 42, 107, 134, 144, 150
Political communication, 11, 40, 76, 105–6, 191
Political marketing, 152–54
  cause, 152
  celebrity endorsements, 153
  comparative advertising, 153
  constituency, 153
Political orientations newspapers, 42
Political reporting, 50
Pradhan Mantri Jan Dhan Yojana, 76
Prakash, Smita, 53
Press Commission, 58
Press Council Act, 60, 67
Press Council of India (PCI), 21, 25–27, 44–45, 53, 57–60, 62–63, 65–67
  duties, 27
  exit polls guidelines, 63
  guidelines 2010, 62–63
  report on paid news, 58–59
Press freedom, 27–28
Press movement, 15
Press theories, 14–16
  Authoritarian Theory, 15
  Communist Theory, 15–16
  Libertarian Theory, 15
  Social Responsibility Theory, 16
Prevention of Terrorism Act (POTA), 133
Print media
  ownership patterns, 26–27
  reach of the, 23–24
Professional publicists and campaigners, 182–84

Propaganda model, 50
'Public interest', 84
Public opinion, 6–12
Public Opinion (book), 10
Public Opinion Quarterly (journal), 10
Public opinion polls, 86–89
　critics of, 86
　Dr Gallup predictions, 86
　guidelines, 86
Public relations (PR), 21
Public sector, disinvestment of, 128
Punj, Balbir, 195

Quantitative research, 87
Quraishi, S.Y., 196

Radical model, 11
Radio in India, 29–30
Radio listenership, 25
Ram Janmabhoomi, 117, 123–24
Raman, Anuradha, 60
Rao, Bhaskar, 123
Rao, K. Chandrashekar, 186
Rao, P.V. Narasimha, 74, 119–20, 125
Rashtriya Janata Dal (RJD), 90
Rashtriya Swayamsevak Sangh (RSS), 148, 167, 168
"Rate cards" or "packages", 22
Rath yatra, 119. *See also* Advani, L.K.
Reader's Digest, 38
Reckitt & Coleman, 112
Reddy, K. Sreenivas, 21, 58, 65
Registrar of Newspaper (RNI), 22
Religious polarization, 90
Religious solidarity, 92
Representation of the People Act, 56, 58, 60, 67
Representative bodies, 3
Republican Party, 107
Revolutionary Socialist, 132
Right to Information (RTI), 154
Roosevelt, Franklin D., 7
Roy Mousumi, 41

Sainath, P., 57, 59
Samajwadi Party, 52, 119, 125, 132, 177
Samta Party, 125

Sardesai, Rajdeep, 51–52, 56, 162, 195
The Saturday Evening Post, 38
Sawaraj, Sushma, 145
Schramm, Wilbur, 14
Secularism vs. pseudo-secularism, 148
Securities and Exchange Board of India (SEBI), 44–45, 26
Self-regulation, 65–66
Seminar, 80
Shah, Amit, 147, 185, 190–91
Sharma, Rajat, 74, 162
Shaw, Donald, 9
'Shehzada'. *See* Gandhi, Rahul
Shekhar, Chandra, 116, 118–20, 122, 124
Shiromani Akali Dal (SAD), 61, 128, 184
Shukla, Rajiv, 195
Siebert, Fred S., 14
Sigal, Leon, 50
Simon Commission, 73
Singh, Ajay, 154
Singh, Arun, 111–12, 126
Singh, Joginder, 127
Singh, Manmohan, 125, 131, 133–34, 190, 194
Singh, S.P., 124
Singh, V.P., 116–22, 125
Social media, 30, 41, 51, 65, 79–80, 85, 151, 154, 165, 168, 170–72, 181, 188, 190–91
　anonymity of, 51
　debatable issue, 30
　female votes, 41
　first-time voters, 154
　impact on voting behaviour, 41
　Modi's comments on, 171
　perceptions, 85–86
　sentiments for Brand Modi, 168
　ubiquity of, 51
　vigorous use of, 154
Social policy, transmission of, 15
Soft Hindutva, 189
Soho Square (O&M), 172
Sridharan, E., 101
Standards of political discourse, deteriorating, 188–95

character assassination, 188
decline in political decorum, 188
personal attacks, 188
religious polarization, 193
The Statesman, 27
Street plays, 168, 174

Taflinger, Richard F., 54
Target rating point (TRP), 81
Tata Global Beverages, 84
Tata Motors, 156
Tata, Ratan, 149
Telecom Regulatory Authority of India (TRAI), 20
Telegraph, 42
Television in India, 28–29
viewership, 24
Telugu Desam Party (TDP), 117
Terrorism in Punjab, 110
Testing the brand, 156
Thakurta, Guha, 55, 58, 62
Thakurta, Paranjoy Guha, 21, 65
The Myth of Objectivity in Journalism, 54
Third-party endorsement, 21
Tiananmen Square Massacre, China, 77
Time, 165
The Times of India, 42
Trinamool Congress, 91, 128
Truman, Harry S., 5
Trump, Donald, 52, 153
Trump-Hillary campaign, 153
Twitter, 30, 41, 52, 79–80, 151, 170–72, 192
'Two-step flow' of communication, 8

United Democratic Front (UDF), 185
United Progressive Alliance (UPA), 39, 64, 99, 107, 129, 132, 134, 144, 148, 150, 163, 186

Upper middle and middle class voter, 94–100
class composition, 95
class-wise party preference, 97
class-wise turnout, 95
preference by caste/community, 98
rural-urban locations wise turnout, 96
turnout of, 95
voters by different class and age groups, 97

Vaishnav, Milan, 83
Vajpayee, Atal Bihari, 82, 115, 126–29, 132–33, 145, 180–81
Vajpayee government, 128–29
Varshney, Ashutosh, 176
Vemula, Rohith, suicide incident, 42
Verghese, B.G., 60
Vishva Hindu Parishad (VHP), 117, 123–24
Voter Verifiable Paper Audit Trail (VVPAT), 89
Voting behaviour, 38–43

Wagle, Nikhil, 61
Wagner, Markus, 13
The Wall Street Journal, 165
The Washington Post, 52
Westminster Electoral System, 131
World Press Freedom Day, 63

Yadav, Akhilesh, 74
Yadav, Lalu Prasad, 119, 127
Yadav, Mulayam Singh, 177
Yadav, Sharad, 126
Yadav, Umlesh, 56
YouTube, 151, 169, 171–72, 175

Zingale, Nancy N., 76